There are numerous books about dreams on the market, but *A Dreamer's Thought Book* is unique, provocative, and unlike anything you might have read about this fascinating topic. Its author, Richard Bargdill, sees dreams as a "school for the soul," one that is both unique and universal, both playful and profound. No matter if you have done dreamwork for years or are a newcomer, you will find novel ways of appreciating your dreams that you never found possible.

Stanley Krippner, PhD
Author, *A Chaotic Life*

A Dreamer's Thought Book: Intriguing Ideas About the Dreaming Process is a wonderful and inspiring book for both professionals and lay people interested in dreamwork. The idea of presenting all this powerful material and information in the form of maxims and aphorisms for every entry is a very creative and helpful format for the reader. One can easily access those maxims that they are interested in and can use the book as a great reference point. The tips for recording dreams and the emphasis given in our night life can arouse one's interest in the dreaming process. I am sure I will recommend this book to my students and clients.

Evgenia T. Georganda, PsyD, ECP
Clinical Psychologist-Psychotherapist
The Hellenic Association for Existential Psychology

Richard Bargdill's latest work is an intimate portrayal of his own decades long journey into the manifold worlds of his dreams. It is a genuinely heuristic venture. Although heuristic refers to the process of "discovering for one's self," Bargdill generously shares the personal insights and principles he has gleaned for others to consider for grasping ever surprising meanings from their own oneiric adventures.

Erik Craig, PhD, Psychologist, Author, and
Past President of the International Association

A Dreamer's Thought Book

Intriguing Ideas about the Dreaming Process

By Richard Bargdill, PhD

University
PROFESSORS PRESS

Colorado Springs, CO
www.universityprofessorspress.com

ISBN (Paperback): 978-1-955737-44-9
ISBN (Hardcover): 978-1-955737-46-3
ISBN (Ebook):   978-1-955737-45-6

University Professors Press
Colorado Springs, CO
www.universityprofessorspress.com

Cover Image by Richard Bargdill
Cover Design adapted by Laura Ross

Table of Contents

Introduction

In college, I attended a series of house parties where people staked out their party positions in certain rooms. There were porch people, a living room crew, and, in my case, kitchen dwellers. My strategy included the thought that almost everybody had to come there, at some point, to refill their beverage. This physical location allowed me to interact with the maximum number of guests, including those I would not just walk up to and introduce myself. My goal was to have as many interesting conversations as possible. This meant that I often used non-sequitur type comments that avoided cliche topics like the weather, sports, or politics. I wanted to catch the attention of the people I spoke to and leave a bit of an impression. I was doing this purposefully to overcome a painful shyness from childhood. Sometimes this approach was successful. The pithy comment that I might have made garnered a familiar saying at that time, which was: "That's pretty funny, you should write it down."

After hearing "write it down" a few times, I decided to take the guests seriously. This initiated a habit of writing down things that I had said that others thought were witty. Soon I just relied on my own judgment, which was much more lenient when it came to deciding if the statement was worthy. This process, which began over 30 years ago, has already led to a book called *An Artist's Thought Book: Intriguing Thoughts about the Artistic Process*, now in its second edition. In that book, I sorted and then collected a series of pithy statements that I called *maxims*. The book has five different topics (poetry, painting, etc.) that concern the artistic process. The maxims were written when I was working on art and suddenly had a thought that inspired me or described what I was trying to do as I made the artwork. Maxims are mostly one-sentence comments, and these art-related ones had an ambiguous, paradoxical, or suggestive quality to them. So, I picked some of my favorites and expounded on the maxim by adding an aphorism. An aphorism is a one- to two-paragraph explanation of the intricacies that are implicated in the much shorter statement. This format is continued in this current book that is based on dreams.

Unlike my previous book, *A Dreamer's Thought Book* has a maxim and an aphorism for every entry, more than 125 individual items. Each passage is about a page long. There are five separate sections covering dream topics: humorous thoughts about dreams; memories and, other capacities we have in dreams, observations about how dreams work; keys to interpreting dreams, and finally, my own theories about what dreams are. This self-contained maxim/aphorism format will allow people to either read straight through the book or, if they choose, randomly select various chapters or individual passages to read in a manner that is conducive to their own interests. Footnotes will appear on the bottom of the page for those who want to do some further reading on the topic. A thorough index is provided so readers can easily find topics that they want to return to.

The following is a brief overview of each chapter. In Chapter 1, we start with some fun thoughts about dreams. Some of the maxims have a witty quality, but then the aphorism accompanying it will fill out details showing that the observation has some merit to it. One of the unique contributions that this book expounds is that we experience "nightmirth." This is a term I coined that suggests our dreams can make us laugh just as much as a nightmare can scare us.

In Chapter 2, we look at how dreams can become confused with memories and reality. I share my experience of prophecies, memories, and the process of déjà vu that occurs when experiences in real life end up matching with things that we have previously dreamed. One of the main themes of this chapter is recognizing dreams that can be easily forgotten, so there are many tips on how to better remember your dreams by setting a mental intention to recall them. Once we have the captured memory of our dream, we then want to record it or tell it to someone else because in the telling of the dream the meaning will often emerge in the very words we use to describe the dream action.

In Chapter 3, we report some observations about the uniqueness of dreams. We will discuss how following your dreams can increase your sense of openness, flexibility, and creativity. We will also cover how following your dreams can enrich your overall life. One of the main themes is that memory, reality, and dreams make up the triple point of the mind. This is the place where history, prophecy, and the present can collide. The past can always be edited; the present only exists in this second although any decision suggests many exits; and the future that we anticipate may not occur in any form that we have forecasted.

In Chapter 4, we get into the meaning of dreams. I suggest that dreams are trying to communicate to us. Dreams can be messages. They can be warnings. They can be commentaries. They can be attempts at telling us to correct behavior in which we have already engaged. One of the main contributions of the book is to suggest that we can compare our dreams to various sayings in our language. These sayings are sometimes called idioms, such as "You are going downhill fast." Dreams, then, visually repeat this message that we might see as a car without brakes going down a hill toward an impossible turn but always picking up speed. Once we break this code, we can interpret some of our dreams quite easily.

In Chapter 5, the theory about what dreams mean takes center stage. I suggest that dreams can often put us in a similar situation in which we have recently put another person. I call this *karmic inversion*: The dream does to us what we have done to others, giving us a real chance to experience the golden rule in reverse. One of the main conclusions of this book is that dreams can provide an individual with extra experience. We, generally, accept that we can learn from movies, books, plays, and musical plots. Dreams are also opportunities to learn about who we are. My conclusion is that dreams are a school for your soul.

Finally, if you have specific questions about a particular dream and want some help understanding it, I have developed a dream service. There, you describe the dream and answer several questions about specific features of your dream. I use the information provided in your answers to give you a written reply. You can find this service at www.dreammetaphors.com.

Chapter 1

Humorous Comments about Dreams

1

I had a dream in which I could speak perfect French, so I know
this ability was locked somewhere in my brain. So, I got a
screwdriver and a hammer. I screwed and whacked,
but it didn't help because I was asleep.

I had a dream when I was learning French in high school or college in which a French person was speaking to me and their French was perfect. The dream-me could understand French perfectly, and yet even in the dream I could not respond with anything but my typical beginner's French. When I woke up, I began to think about how this should be the case. In the dream, the French speaker was fluent, which means that somewhere in my brain" I have the ability to speak French in this same way. Otherwise, the French would have been incorrect or incomprehensible. This was the moment I realized much of what we know, or can learn easily, might already be there as potential in the collective unconscious—a repository of human knowledge that can be accessed through dreams.

Recently, there have been a number of cases[1] where a person with an accidental blow to the head has awakened to find that they have a "special" and previous undiscovered talent: a man who suddenly can play and write piano music, a woman who can speak fluently a foreign language that she never studied.[2] This magical appearance of talent is what I was thinking about as I woke from my French dream. Maybe all the information and abilities are already in our grasp, and only our "confidence" and our situation can let them out.

---

[1] https://uproxx.com/life/derek-amato-musical-savant/
[2] https://www.sciencealert.com/people-keep-waking-up-from-head-injuries-speaking-a-different-language

2

Dreams are the mind's garbage disposal.

When we look at the contents of our dreams, especially over a series of dreams, it quickly becomes apparent that certain events, images, or themes from our ordinary lives get sprinkled into the dreams. This has led some researchers to believe that the dreaming process has something to do with the memory process. I distinctly remember that after watching the movie *Gladiator,* a night or two later I dreamed a wild tiger appeared to attack me. The movie contains scenes with lions, so the appearance of tigers in my dream seemed to be some homage to the recent viewing of the movie. Large wildcats are not a common image in my dreams, so this reappearance clearly shows us that dreams do contain recent events, whether those are actual or virtual.

When we have any dream, then, we should be looking to connect recent dream images to recent waking experiences. I have noticed that waking images do not always happen in dreams the very night they occurred but can be two to three days removed, although it is not impossible for them to occur the same night. The dream can even blend together—like a garbage disposal—a variety of different aspects into one narrative. Freud called this combination of elements *condensation,*[3] as in two things condensed into one. Any condensation in a dream means that this dream was worthy of scrutiny.

3

Dreams are the acceptance of the unconscious; not only is there suspension of disbelief, there is often the suspension of doubt.

"The suspension of disbelief" is a concept that originated in the study of theater. The idea was that for the audience to get the most out of the performance, a viewer had to set aside their overly rational analytic side so that they could become immersed in the story. In other words, if a viewer is concentrating on every single "plot hole" or statistical impossibility, then they would be jerked out of the magic of the show.

What makes dreams so adventurous is that they typically start with a suspension of disbelief so powerful that you do not even recognize you are not in reality. The dream surroundings may look like an actual

---

[3] https://www.ncbi.nlm.nih.gov/pmc/articles/PMC534695/

place that you have lived before, but something is "off" about the image. It is not your identical home. Sometimes two former spaces are combined (e.g., condensation), such as a childhood bedroom and college dorm room smashed together.

None of this pulls us out of the dream at that moment and only appears "weird" to us upon waking. *Suspension of disbelief* means that we appear to have "predictive judgment" or "forethought" removed from our tool bag. In some way, within the dream we are truly in the moment, sucked into the action of the dream so deeply that we do not anticipate the consequences of our actions. The dream may be the one place where we are truly in the *here and now*. If we become aware of any of this, we usually wake up immediately.

4

There is good indication that my dreams were the Ancient Greek reality.

When historians talk about "rational" thinking in the West, there is a particular philosopher with whom they associate the beginning of rational thought: Heraclitus. One of his famous statements is that "You never stick your foot into the same river," the idea being that the water you touch today will be further down the river tomorrow and out to the sea by Thursday. Prior to Heraclitus, the world of the Ancient Greeks, to whom we owe our rational lineage, was more closely connected to the ideas found in what we call "mythology."

Sometimes we forget that those Greeks would not have considered it mythology at all: It was their worldview. If we believed what they did, we would call it religion! "Worldview" means that this was how they understood the way the world is organized. There were Fates that determined factors about an individual's life. There were several gods competing with and antagonizing other gods in a larger drama. They used human beings as toys and pets and ego boosters. The world was full of magic powers, dangerous beasts, and sexual infatuation. In our relatively mundane lives in Western civilization, our dreams are one of the few places that we can experience this worldview, where we are the main character in an epic adventure. Most of our forays into these mythic experiences are as a passive viewer of commercial movies.

5

My dreams have gotten so shallow they look like a reflecting pool.

Dreams show us our concerns, and yet they alter the landscape so that we do not see parallels easily. They transport us out of our real-life geography; however, the psychological situation of our lives is usually revealed in an accurate fashion. One way to understand the dream's meaning is to disregard the setting and merely concentrate on the emotional quality of the dream, especially if it is a common dream theme. For example, it is common to have dreams where one is trying to do a simple action, such as leave the house on time. This action is thwarted by a series of issues: a forgotten packed lunch, an unexpected phone call, missing car keys, etc.

When looking at the dream, we could be distracted by all the unreal aspects: the house is not my real house, I am younger than I actually am, I may have a dream-partner who is not my real-life partner, I might not be in the same city I live in, etc. These are not the details to get caught up in! The dream's meaning is most readily found in the emotion of being frustrated, and not just frustrated in some minor way. It most likely means there are deeper and profound levels where you feel frustrated (e.g., not living up to your potential). If you follow the money in a political investigation, then in dreams you follow the emotion. Thus, the question this dream raises is: What is frustrating you now and what, in general, is frustrating you in life?

6

From neurotic to erotic! Every shy person's dream.

Psychiatrist Medard Boss suggests there is a higher level of freedom available in your dreams than might seem possible to you in your waking life.[4] Of course, we can also feel a higher level of oppression in nightmares. Certainly, some dreams provide us with powers that are beyond human capability, such as our physical bodies flying without machinery. This common dream shows us a physical representation of freedom and is often interpreted as a time in the person's waking life when they are "flying high." But another very important aspect of freedom is the acceptance of the self that is shown in romantic dreams, usually with anonymous figures.

A common dream theme includes dream descriptions like "I know she was my girlfriend in the dream." An anonymous figure of the opposite sex was considered by Carl Jung to be an "anima" or "animus,

[4] Boss, M. (1957). *The analysis of dreams* (J. Pomerans, Trans.). Philosophical Library.

female aspects of the male personality or the male parts of the female personality. In the dream, this is meant to show the dreamer how to better balance themself by adding complementary qualities to smooth over the dominant qualities contained in one's gender.

In any case, for a shy person, dreams can feature figures full of acceptance—our dream lovers. They can provide us with some confidence that there are entities out there that value us, find us attractive, and see our potential. When we feel neurotic and unlovable during waking times, our erotic dream partners show us that there is more to ourselves than we think.

7

Dreams are your own personal Rorschach. You can see in them what you see through you.

The Rorschach inkblot test was once a frequently used psychological test. An assessor would present a series of ambiguous images to a client, who would be asked to describe what they see. Surprisingly, the responses would greatly vary between different persons looking at the same stimulus. The test had a specific set of cards that were shown in order. If there was a "common" answer to a certain card, that answer would be called a popular response. However, many times persons would see novel items, or see movement where others might have seen the image as being still. Other more "empirical" tests (e.g., MMPI) are now more often utilized, but many clinicians who assess with the Rorschach believe that it was much more useful for understanding how a person made sense of the ambiguous nature of reality.

Dreams are much more in the vein of an inkblot; we cannot say what an image *means* for everyone. The dream is personalized. In order to find the right "interpretation" for the dreamer, we have to help them find something in the story that resonates with them personally. The dream interpreter can only offer suggestions and hope that the dreamer might have that "Ah-ha" moment where the offering rings that bell.

8

My last dream was about wine-making and espionage.

Both our imagination and our dreams put us into unfamiliar situations. In the waking imagination, we can place ourselves into contexts and then create various scenarios that allow us to anticipate future opportunities. By imagining these outcomes, we gain the experience of trying out potential actions and seeing the likely result of this behavior. And this all occurs in the safe space of our mind. In a dream, we are "placed" into a foreign scenario in order to see what we do and "how we like it."

The imaginative realm retains a sense of 'rationality' to it since it is *we* who engage in building the conditions during a "daydream." If we do not like the outcome of our imagined actions, we can always call for a "do-over" and go back to a certain point and pick up from that spot. Then continue the storyline in a different direction (much like a computer program that has an Undo button).

Since dreams do include information from the previous day(s), one can think of a dream as a simulation meant to take us through some overlooked step; it is a form of education (experience giving). If dreams are intentional simulations, then they are not the same as the daydreams we experience since in daydreams the person is cognizant of creating the scenario and judging the outcome. Many dreams do not give us happy endings but rather rouse the dreamer from sleep because of tragedy; our only do-over happens once we are awake.

9

Dreams are the art gallery of the mind.

One night I had a powerful dream in which I had a painting in an important art gallery on opening night. In my waking life, I am an amateur artist who shows work occasionally. As I walked into the show, I was wondering about the quality of my art piece and how it might look compared to the other works displayed. As I searched for my piece, I was in awe of the works of the other artists displayed on the walls. Each piece seemed to one-up the previous pieces. The works were meaningful and visually complex. I became somewhat nervous that my own work would be inferior to the work I was seeing. Eventually, I found my own piece. I was thrilled to see that it was a good fit, so this turned into a happy dream.

The best surprise of the dream was when I woke up. It was at this time I realized that my painting in the dream was not anything I had painted before. It was not a completed painting of mine that happened to appear in the dream. Then, I also realized that none of the paintings by the "other" artists were paintings that I recognized from books I had looked at or galleries I had visited. In other words, ALL the paintings in the dream were MY paintings. I had made these paintings up! And they were great. By the time I realized this, I could no longer remember the paintings in their depth and beauty. But since then, I have added a sketch book to my nightstand so that if any art appears in future dreams, I am ready to capture it.

10

It is often difficult when you realize that maybe your dreams ultimately won't help you get out of this jam!

Dreams can often relay messages to you that something is amiss. One common dream that Carl Jung identified is being inside a malfunctioning vehicle (e.g., brakes do not work), or your driver is drunk, or there is no driver at all but the vehicle is moving. Jung associated the vehicle with our "drive" or motivation.[5]. So, we can ask ourselves: Am I "driven" toward something without the ability to stop myself (e.g., addictive behavior)? Am I following the lead of a person who is out of control or impaired (i.e., drunk). Am I in a situation where there is nobody who is really in charge?

Jung also thought that every character in a dream was an aspect of you. There is no "boss" or anyone else to pin responsibility on; you are the only one who can actually face up to your problems. The dream is for you. Hence, the dream often does not solve your problem, but it can make you aware of the situation. You can try to deny it or assume the problem is "external," but the only solution is an internal one. When most people have the "car without brakes" dream, they will assume it is about their actual car (a literal interpretation) rather than see it as a sign that their life is out of control.

11

All my dreams are mixed metaphors.

---

[5] Mahoney, M. F. (1972). *The meaning in dreams and dreaming. (pp. 180-182).* Citadel Press.

In the early days of psychology there was a thought that "mixing metaphors" was an example of an unstable mind. The patient might say "It's raining cat skins!" instead of saying either: "It's raining cats and dogs" or "There's more than one way to skin a cat." This is considered a *contamination* because the person was unable to keep the two well-known aphorisms apart and instead made an incoherent one.

Freud recognized that the condensing of two separate images was an indicator of an "important" dream and that the dream should be analyzed. A condensation occurs in dreaming when one thing magically turns into another similar object. Common examples might include a familiar person (e.g., mother) turning into another kindred person (wife). For Freud, this condensation[6] indicated that a problem that once existed with one's mother was now also repeating itself with one's wife (a repetition compulsion). If this repeating complex was not brought to light, the same relationship issues would arise for the dreamer in both relationships.

One of the best ways to address dreams like this is to ask: "How is what happened in the dream similar to what I'm going through in my life now?" Another question might be "How is my conflict with X (e.g., mom) similar to problems with Y (wife)?" Dreams are largely about present concerns—even if they seem to be about historic events and characters.

12

Dreams are stories started without context. If dreams were a child, you'd tell them to start from the beginning.

Sometimes it is difficult to remember the entirety of a dream that can seem like it has a long back story we cannot remember upon waking. In fact, if we equate REM (rapid eye movement) sleep precisely with dreaming, the final REM period during sleep can reach up to an hour long. So potentially a long dream could be an hour long, which is not considered if there is a distortion of time when dreaming. It is not likely that one minute of dreaming is the same as one minute of waking. Those who write down their dreams know that a few minutes of dreaming can take the awake-me 20 minutes to describe.

---

[6] Freud, S. (1953). *On Dreams* (J. Strachey, Trans.). W.W. Norton. (Original work published 1901)

With that being said, dreams do insert you into situations that to the waking mind seem to be contextless. It is very common to hear a dreamer start with the phrase, "I find myself in...." as if there is no backstory to what happens. Plop! My dream-me is inserted into this situation and has to do something. Interestingly, in most dreams, the dream-me almost always knows something about what they are up against, seems able to form a coherent plan, and is quick to make a decision that moves the plot forward. These actions either make the dream end well or produce consciousness due to dream tragedy. Oddly enough, it is only the awake-me that cares about the back story.

13

*I've been having philosophical dreams, but even in the dream
I'm not taking notes.*

Many dreams can put you into extraordinary circumstances, but you can also be placed in quite mundane situations. A common dream is to return to high school as a student. One way to think about these dreams is to ask if you are in a position in waking life where you have to humble yourself to the level of a beginner. As adults we want to "know it all" and something simple like not knowing how to use the newest computer app can put us in a situation where we feel like a student again.

At other times, we may dream of being a teacher in school even though that is not our profession. This may indicate that we took the time to help a person in need and gave some friendly advice to a coworker. Possibly, the dream is encouraging us to interact with a person that could benefit from our experienced point of view. If you view teachers as boring, the dream might be reprimanding you for being preachy in your lessons to others.

Very few of my dreams include situations where the classroom activity includes a long lecture. Dreams seem to be action oriented, but I have had a few that did contain talks. In each case, I did not take any notes on what was said. This can suggest that in that moment, I was feeling confident that I understood what is transpiring for me in the "school of life."

14

I'm always impressed by other people's art in my dreams.

We have discussed how most of the art in your dreams are creations of your own mind (see #9), not art of other people or a known piece of art (e.g., Mona Lisa); rather, it is in fact your dream art. It is not always easy to retrieve art from a dream, but it is worth trying. I once had a dream about a song being played on the radio. It was the first time I heard the song and it was thrilling. At the end of the song, the radio personality announced that this was the latest song by Kris Kristopherson. I woke up shortly after this and was thinking that this was a great song. I decided I was going to look for that work in Kristopherson's catalog when it dawned on me that this was not a song by him. By then I could barely remember any of the lyrics or melody.

A secondary issue in this type of dream is being impressed by other people at the expense of under-valuing your own work. In other words, this is a call to put more effort into your own projects and make sure you are carving out the time in your busy schedule to do the things that bring you joy. Repeated dream themes like this usually speak to a psychological "theme"; Freud called this a *complex*.[7] This complex is something worth reflecting on. Someone having such a repeated dream might want to ask: Why do you have such an inferiority complex about your work but seem eager to heap praise on other people's work? Confidence, after all, is sexy.

15

Dreams from a foreign bed end up hanging around in my head.

When visiting friends, I often enjoyed this one room where the temperature was quite cold (62°F). The hosts first put me there out of necessity, but on other visits when warmer rooms were available, I declined them when they were offered. I noticed that in the cooler room, in a foreign bed, I would have incredibly numerous intricate dreams.[8] The cool temperature seemed to help in this. Remembering a dream means becoming temporarily conscious (you must wake up). The cold temperature that is being experienced when changing position most likely means that consciousness is more likely to be reached frequently, helping the retention of the dream.

---

[7] Freud, S. (2010). *The interpretation of dreams* (J. Strachey, Trans.). Basic Books (original work published 1900)
[8] https://www.tuck.com/sleep/temperature-for-sleep/

While many of us do not sleep as well in a foreign bed, simply because we are not in familiar territory, this can stimulate the memory of multiple dreams. People generally will remember the last dream of the night as that is the one that is most obvious right before consciousness occurs for the day. The experienced dreamer who is recording their dreams will find that dreams do occur throughout the night; in fact, it is quite possible to have four or five dreams of some length during the night. It is helpful to have a notepad next to your bed to at least make a few notes about the content of the dream. Without any notes, one dream (usually the last one of the night) will erase the prior dreams, and those earlier dreams could actually be more significant.

16

I'm estranged from him in waking life but in my dreams,
we are still friends.

Dreams give us a chance to reconnect with friends with whom we might not be on speaking terms. I often find that dreams return us to a time when we are not estranged from a certain friend. We are still in a time of cooperation, and the friendship is pure. We trust each other and work toward the resolution that the dream requires. Because of this, I believe that dreams can actually push us towards reconciliation with that person—similar to the "empty chair technique" that allows us to speak our piece to someone who is not there.

In a similar vein, I have had dreams about former schoolteachers who have positively impacted me and now appear in a dream of mine 20 years later. A couple of times, I was inspired to reach out to these teachers and tell them that I appreciated their help, concern, and style. Many people have helped us along the way and do not even know the positive impact they have had on us. If you call someone and recount your gratitude for their past actions, you will likely hear them say: "Wow, you don't know how much I needed to hear that today." You may have done equally impactful gestures for others, and your moments of gratitude might be ten years in the future or only ever arrive to you in a dream.

17

My dream muses always seem to think I'm talented.

For me, a common dream that I have had many times is that I have the support of a lover who is unknown to the awake-me. The lover is of the opposite sex and is not my real-life partner. In other words, it is an anonymous female character who is felt to be my love interest. For years, I called these women my "muses" because they often have given me support in my dreams or told me they expected more of myself. One of my favorite comments from a muse was that I was only one of her many lovers, but I was rising in her preference rankings. Yet still, I was not there yet.

Carl Jung uses the term *anima*[9] for a female who visits a male dreamer at night (*animus* for a male muse). The anima/animus, according to Jung, demonstrates how to balance out our personality by giving us behavioral examples. The anima is not a "different" person—that's why we do not recognize our lover—but is a loving part of our own psyche that is trying to tell us how to act or in this case offer us the support that may be our waking ego. Our task is then to integrate the behavior of the feminine (or vice versa) into our masculine personality. My dream of supportive lovers would suggest that I should be more accepting of myself and others, tone down the criticism, and see myself and others as projects that are starting to show some progress.

18

Dream: Light shines on me when I sleep.

All kinds of great things have come out of dreams. Dreams have helped people invent new things, solve science problems, create new forms of math, as well as inspire numerous works of art. In the footnote link below, you will see that some of the famous scientific discoveries[10] have occurred from dreams. including: the periodic table, the formation of the benzene ring, and the development of string theory mathematics.

Problem solving seems to be a two-part process: the first task is intensely thinking about things when you are awake. This entails grinding on a problem so thoroughly that you have left no "conscious" stone unturned. When the solution is not found that way, the second

[9] Jung, C.G. (1974). *Dreams* (R.F.C. Hall, Trans.; p.128). Princeton University Press. (Original work published 1909)
[10] https://www.famousscientists.org/7-great-examples-of-scientific-discoveries-made-in-dreams/

phase of problem solving is not thinking about it. We have to put the problem aside for a period of time. By letting go of hunting for the answer, we allow the solution to show up. Frequently, our summoned solutions will arise when the mind is involved in minor activities like driving a familiar route or washing the dishes, and while dreaming. Both parts are important to the outcome; focusing on the question while awake allows the unconscious to know the intention is to find the answer. Letting consciousness release this focus opens the portal so that the answer can pop through.

19

Dreams are the sample platter of other souls' existences.

Dreams are filled with strangers, but you "seem" to know them quite well in the dream scenario. Jung suggests that non-romantic strangers in dreams are "parts" of your personality, so that a fight you have with a stranger is an internal conflict where you are fighting with yourself.[11] The stranger represents a different perspective that you might not be fully recognizing as having some traction in your mind. Thus, the stranger's actions should be reflected upon and integrated.

I have a different view of strangers. If our dreaming process is tied to memory consolidation, then dream-strangers might be actual strangers we see on the streets or other common areas who get recorded into our dreams. We know that much of the data of our lives gets stored somewhere in the memory system. People under hypnosis are able to recover incredible details of events that they just glimpsed for a second or two. I suggest that strangers are subconscious projections of who we take those people to be.

Other folks have said that dream-strangers are actually your friends from "past lives." The reason they appear in our dreams is that they are trying to help us make a good decision in waking life. We, however, do not recognize them as real persons any longer.

20

Dreams are like reality. They never tell the truth—at least initially.

---

[11] Freud, S. (2010). *The interpretation of dreams* (J. Strachey, Trans.). Basic Books (original work published 1900)

One of Freud's great insights was that dreams cannot be taken at face value. Dreams are not literal narratives. If your car's brakes do not work in a dream, it does not mean you need to take your car to a real-life mechanic. Dreams are metaphorical. The exact plot of the dream, what Freud called the "manifest content," is not actually the message of the dream. To get the message (latent content), one must loosely compare the events of the dream with the actual experiences of the awake-me and look for similarities (e.g., no brakes = you cannot stop yourself). The message tends to click when the action of the dream resembles something occurring in waking life. You will often realize you have the right interpretation when you experience an "Ah-ha" moment.

In this way, both reality and dreams only reveal partial truths to us, and we have to figure out the rest. In real life, we discover as we age that the truth we are told is basically an interpretation of events often told by the victors. Holy days have been completely stripped of their original meaning. Most of the stories we tell our children from the very beginning of their lives all turn out to be fabrications. These stories are fun for the adults because they, too, were tricked by these stories that turn out to be no more real than that dream you had at night.

21

If you are having powerful dreams, you must be ready for powerful scenes.

There are times when our dreams are very vivid and complex and other times when the dreams seem to be mundane. Carl Jung thought that dreams balance our psyches so that when we are too "high" or over-confident, dreams[12] might bring us down either by scaring us (nightmare) or showing us in inadequate control (in the backseat of a driverless moving car). On the other hand, dreams can bring us up or boost our confidence when we are low (meeting a hero of yours in dream).

A common dream that can do both at once is a "flying" dream. Here, the dream-me has the extraordinary power of being able to fly without machinery. The body flies like a plane, and we get a bird's-eye view of the landscape. These dreams can suggest that right now we are "flying high" or seeing the whole picture. But anyone who has had such a dream will recognize that shortly after the novelty of flying wears off,

---

[12] Mahoney, M. F. (1972). *The meaning in dreams and dreaming* (pp.179–186) Citadel Press.

concerns arise: "Am I getting too high up?" and "How am I going to land safely?" These thoughts usually lead the dream to come to an end. The dream idiom serves as a warning: "What goes up must come down."

22

Happy to find the damage that happened to me in my night dreams was only psychological.

Many people have awakened from dreams only to breathe a sigh of relief that the actions that took place were not real events—at least on this plane of existence. It is possible that our dreams are the realities of versions of ourselves in parallel universes. But the relief we feel is that those events that felt so real a second ago are nothing that we have to deal with now. One time, without realizing I had dreamed I was late for an important upcoming meeting, I found myself in the shower at 3 am. Only after I was done washing did I notice through the bathroom window that it was still dark outside. I realized that it could not be waking time, so I dried off and tried to return to sleep (to no avail).

It is not just about being fooled by dreams, which occasionally happens; but we can also be embarrassed by our dream-me's behavior. Freud used the term "displacement" to refer to actions that your awake-me would never do, at least, publicly. Jung used the term "shadow[13]" in recognizing that the dream-me often gravely misbehaves when compared to one's awake-me. However, your shadow could also show up in waking life when you are stressed, exhausted or physically ill. Both displacement and shadow dreams require some attention because they reveal an unpleasant aspect of our personality—although not necessarily an aspect we should try to eliminate. These dreams will receive further attention throughout this book.

23

When you don't drink, you end up dreaming.

Each person's dreaming cycle is a little bit different. Personal habits can help you retain dreams, and other habits can interfere with dream retention. Good habits that help dream recall include going to bed at the

---

[13] Green, T. A (1979). C.G. Jung's theory of dreams. In B.B. Wolman (Ed.) *Handbook of dreams: Research, theories and applications.* (pp. 298-318) Van Nostrand Reinhold, Co.

same time and having a consistent amount (hours) of sleep. We know that REM[14] (Rapid Eye Movement = dream) sleep can occur up to four times in an average night's sleep (eight hours). Non-REM cycles are approximately 90 minutes and proceed each dream cycle. REM sleep increases over the night, with the first period being about 10 minutes and last occurring about 50 minutes prior to waking up for the day. A person with consistent sleep patterns increases chances of remembering their dreams. Also, intentionally saying to yourself that "I want to remember my dreams" is another great habit.

Habits that might interfere with dream remembering include moderate to heavy alcohol use. This does not mean no dreams occur, but the likelihood of remembering them decreases. Waking up to music is another bad practice of dream remembering because even if you have a dream in the morning, the music will take your mind away from the dream and into the lyrics of the song. Finally, any use of sleeping medicine also inhibits the memories of your dreams. To some extent, you do have to wake up to remember a dream, and obviously the point of sleeping medicines is to prevent that from happening.

24

Dreams are kind of the cream filling stuffed inside us.

Dreams have many purposes and once you learn how to understand them, you will find they are one of the best parts of your day! Dreams can act as commentaries that attempt to get you to reconsider previous actions. For example, a dream might do to you in the dream what you did to another in reality.

Dreams can solve problems. Sleep acts as a break from conscious thinking, so when something moves from the front burner to the back burner, there can be a sudden insight that provides an immediate solution.

Dreams can get us to reflect on our relationships. Dreams are rarely "otherless." Most of the time they contain people we know or unfamiliar people that are in a relationship with us: "hypothetical people." Dreams then can point us to trouble spots in interpersonal affairs.

Dreams can warn you about planned behavior. If you consider doing something harsh, do not be surprised if the dream that night shows you the possible consequences of that action but with you as the recipient.

---

[14] Van de Castle, R.L. (1994) *Our dreaming mind.* (pp. 228-235). Ballantine Books.

Dreams can allow us to communicate with people who are no longer on the living plane. Dead relatives often appear in our dreams, and their interactions with us are most likely lessons that we can still learn from.

Dreams can provide prophecy, occasionally predicting the future. My few experiences of this have only resulted in "déjà vu" moments and nothing I could see ahead of time to take advantage of.

25

A cat may have nine lives but if you count the number of deaths
I've had in my dreams, I'm on life 1000.

There used to be this old wife's tale that if you ever experienced death in a dream that you would die in real life! Fortunately, that is not true in my experience since I have died hundreds of times in my dreams. And I did not always wake up before I was dead in the dream. I lay there for a while before I realized I was dead. Most of these dream scenarios are not something that I would likely encounter in waking life. So what could a death in a dream mean?

Like the Death card in a tarot deck, death in a dream can indicate that something important to you is coming to an end. Often seniors in college will have a dream where they are climbing a mountain; nearing the summit, they take their eyes off the trail to look down at the sights and slip and fall to their supposed death. This indicates both the end of college and also not feeling fully prepared for the next stage of life. Death can indicate that something is metaphorically "killing" you–maybe a relationship or a habit–and hence there is unhealthy drama in your life. Death might also mean that you have come to a dead end, and although you may not be able to admit it in real life, you can already see that something in your life is going nowhere. These are just some of the possible meanings for death in a dream. The dreamer has to choose which message is being conveyed at a particular time.

26

If I'm getting all the sex I need in my dreams, why chase it in reality?

Having sex in a dream can have many meanings, just like experiencing death. Freud famously said that dreams are "overdetermined,"[15] which means that there are multiple possible symbolic meanings for any dream action. Although Freu, himself became fixated on dream-sex, especially in forbidden relationships (e.g., mother–son) and somewhat surprisingly saw these as literal desires. Freud's preoccupation with dream-sex as real sexual urges may seem an overreach in today's "sexually liberated" West, but sexual repression was a main feature of Freud's Victorian era. My assertion is that dreams use well-known sayings called idioms, and that there are numerous idioms that have a sexual connotation that are actually not sexual. For example, the idiom "getting into bed with someone" means an unholy partnership that can have nothing to do with sex. So, I strongly disagree with Freud on this point.

Alternative interpretations of sex can mean someone who "turns you on" intellectually. How many times have we said or heard the phrase "I could just kiss you now" when referring to a friend or comrade? Dreams are typically visual mediums and often use "shortcut" imagery to get points across, and sex is an easy way to communicate close connection.

27

You can wake up screaming due to a nightmare.
Today, I woke up laughing due to nightmirth!

"Nightmirth" is my term for the times you wake up from a dream because you're laughing. While we are much more familiar with a dream that wakes us up screaming or from terror, dreams can also be funny. It is actually surprising that we do not find most of the situations amusing since dreams allow us to suspend disbelief and go along with the surreal details of the situation. The strange part of this suspension of disbelief is that we can also lose most of our sense of humor. Certainly, nightmirth is rarer than nightmares, so we should really pay attention to when it happens.

Generally, what makes something funny is that we expect something to occur or someone to make a particular statement in keeping with the context, and then that expectation is violated. Dreams

---

[15] Freud, S. (1961). *Beyond the pleasure principle* (J. Strachey, Trans.). (pp.8–9). W. W. Norton.

often have us in bewildering situations where we have no idea what to expect, and this might be one of the reasons humor is not so prevalent; it is not easy for us to anticipate the actions coming.

Hence when a dream does produce laughter, part of reviewing that dream might include what was expected and how this dream distorted that expectation. Maybe more important is how I am expecting something in waking life that may not turn out the way I want. Children often complain about the "unfairness" of life because what you get is not what you want.

28

Dreams for sale. Get the original notes of a handwritten dream. If you don't dream, you can buy a dream from me cheap!

In order to capture my dreams, I have a pen with a light on the tip and a notebook next to my bed. I have also had to make a deal with my partner to get the side of the bed that allows me to write with my right hand–no easy bargain. When I have a dream at night, I roll over and write down a few notes about the dream. If I have a dream about a sinking ship at sea and hunting a white whale, I will at least jot down "Moby Dick" and possibly "broken boat." Then I go back to bed. Often, I will have another dream in the early morning and jot that down before getting into the shower. Those notes buy me some time before I have to make a full account of the dream.

Once I have recorded the dream, I generally put a slash through the dream notes so I know it has been recorded. The wild part is that the handwriting is only legible based on the degree of alertness that I had when writing. So, the sheet of paper when completely full has the appearance of being written by someone who is mentally unhealthy—maybe someone who has multiple personalities! I have often thought of trying to package these sheets with some nice envelopes, some lavender scents, and trying to offer them as dream charms for those who cannot remember their dreams. Hopefully, the notes of 10+ dreams from a super-seasoned dreamer placed under your pillow will spark a dream for you!

29

My dream is stretching its legs. The best thing you can do is take a dream for a walk.

By "taking a dream for a walk," I mean speaking to someone else about the dream. This is sometimes called the *dream work*. If you can find an empathic partner who is willing to listen to your dreams and whose dreams you are willing to entertain, then this is something that you should take advantage. Sadly, we rarely find someone who is as interested in our dreams as we are. But the meaning of dreams can often be found if the speaker listens to their own description of the dream while speaking to someone else. So, if you cannot tell someone about your dream, or are not able to write them down, at least try to verbally record them on a voice recorder.

While verbalizing your dream, look for "double entendres" in your word choice. That is, places where the word you picked has a potential double meaning. An example: a dream in which a person is involved in a car "accident." While an accident can refer to a "crash" or a major mistake, it also might be referring to behavior that was intended to produce one outcome and instead produced a different, possibly much better, outcome. Not all accidents are bad. My experience suggests that dreams use the "most obvious" visual material, almost like unconscious shorthand, to relate the larger picture—in this case to draw attention to the fact an accident occurred yesterday. That accident may be an accidental discovery, an accidental finding, or a serendipitous outcome, and not necessarily a major mistake.

30

I still haven't figured out this dream. I'm going to put it on the back burner of my dream oven.

As much as I would like to think that I understand at least the basic meaning of every dream I have, that is simply not the truth. Just as every day has some ebbs and flows so do dreams. They seem to have different scenes in them that are addressing one thing, but then dreams have the ability to "teleport" our dream-me directly into another scene with little to no logical connection. Sometimes upon reflection we can make sense of how these two sections interrelate, but frequently it appears to be nonsensical.

As a general feature, dreams are often messages from ourselves to ourselves. So, when I cannot find the thread of meaning to a dream, I often contemplate it for a bit and then try to let it settle on the back burner of my mind. If I have not come up with some way to connect it to my waking life, sometimes I will review as much as I can remember of that dream prior to sleep and ask my unconscious mind to clarify the dream with this night's new dream. Before I go to sleep, I will say, "Help me understand last night's dream about __ with a dream tonight." This is often very effective.

A series of dreams can reveal that there is a theme to what is happening that one may not gather in a single dream. A day's events can easily erase what one was concerned with at night. Thus, reviewing one's dream journal after a couple of inexplicable dreams is a great practice.

31

Nap dreams can be particularly strange because you have
a half a day of bullshit in the dream compactor.

Some people who are not frequent nappers have found that their dreams when napping are particularly potent. A napper is probably more likely to remember their dreams because of the short period of the nap. If the nap is approximately 45–90 minutes, the dream is ending as the same time as the nap. While 90 minutes is the average time to get to REM sleep, a nap may get there quicker since the falling-asleep period (entering non-REM 2) is drastically cut down by exhaustion.

My hypothesis as to why nap dreams are so strange is threefold: first, the dream takes place in an unusual sleep setting: on the couch instead of their bed; or if the napper is in their bed, there may be unusual light and higher temperatures that would not typically be there at night. Second, the person has set a timer in their unconscious mind that compresses any dream action. We know that we can awaken (with some practice) at almost the exact time we want. People often awaken one or two minutes before their alarms. This means that the dreams during a nap are more likely to be similar to the first dreams of the night which are the briefest and often described as more ethereal. Third, night dreams have a complete day's material to work with. In a napping dream, the unconscious is working on a half a day's material that has not been fully digested by the awake-me. Hence, like exercising after you just ate, the nap dream can be strange since it is like unconscious indigestion.

32

Jimmy Carter once said he hoped for the day

when he behaved morally in his dreams. But I wish to never be
embarrassed by anything I do in my dreams.

Carl Jung had the idea of the "shadow,"[16] and Freud spoke similarly about displacement. Both concepts can refer to an unpleasant action you do in your dream that you would "never" do in reality. Jung's shadow concept included the idea that we do not really want to eliminate our shadow's behavior (as Jimmy Carter wants to do); rather, we should recognize what this evil double (doppelgänger) is doing in the dream could be a useful action for our awake-me personality.

Usually, we are repulsed by the shadow-me in our dreams, but if we were forced to give the shadow-me a compliment for its behavior, it might sound something like this: "You are tenacious; I'll give you that." Or "You definitely gave them a piece of your mind." Or "They probably won't mess with you again." For Jung, the shadow's behavior (often an over-the-top action) is trying to encourage us to exhibit behaviors that are more protective of our personalities. So, if your awake-me takes on the work of other people frequently, the shadow dream-me tells people "no" quite forcefully.

Shadows can appear while we are in awake-me mode but generally make an appearance only when we are tired, jet lagged, or feeling ill. Oftentimes others react to this little-seen aggressive part of our personality. Some will say "What's gotten into you?" Rather than retreat and apologize too much for our behavior, we might want to adopt a more refined version of those actions.

33

Dreaming is school for your soul.

The awake world recognizes the three dimensions of space (height, width, length) + time. People have speculated on what a 4-dimensional + time world would be like. I would like to put forth that the dream world shows us how this world operates. I am suggesting that dreaming is school for one's soul. In dreams we learn what to expect when and if we get to 5 dimensions (4D + time). Thus, dreaming is an evolutionary practice.

In our waking world, we experience space as more stable than time. Each day, our bodies are a little bit older, but the changes are barely

---

[16] von Franz, M. L., & Boa, F. (1984). *The way of the dream.* Shambhala Publications.

noticeable to us. Slow-developing behavior sometimes can be witnessed with time-lapse recordings that reveal these minute changes. I propose that in dreaming *time* is the dominant feature: In dreams, two different periods of life are often condensed into one space. This is most noticeable in architecture when dream-buildings contain aspects of a childhood place intermixed with a college-based place. Hence, the dream gives us a clue as to *when* it might be commenting about. In dreaming, we also have lurches in time. One moment in the dream, I am in my room and the next second, I am standing on the streets of Paris. In some dreams, I am in my fifties, in other cases I am in my twenties. Time is much more fluid in dreams.

My assertion is that our dreams are a practice for how reality is different once we get to the higher 4th dimension. There, quite possibly, we will encounter a free range of time which is soul school for the future-you.

Chapter 2

Memory, Perception, and Abilities

34

*Dreams are a form of play! Once we get "too old" for make believe,
our dreams take over that creative action.*

When we are young, we have a wild imagination. We can entertain
ourselves with objects that do not even closely resemble the things we
represent them to be. I recall my young son playing with school erasers
as if they were spaceships or cars. Many of these early mental activities
of young children end up becoming internal dialogue for the adult. At
first our minds need props and scratch paper so that we can visualize
many of our scholastic problems. However, after a while almost
everything that we have to do we can "do in our heads."

   Dreams appear to be a place where this sense of play goes as we age.
After we have been frequently told that it is time to "put that away and
be serious," it is our dreams that maintain our sense of playfulness.
Babies spend most of their time in dreaming-sleep, and as we age we
dream less. I always imagine dreaming as the loading of software into
the human mind. I recall that as a child I had a dream in which spoken
words appeared, and I seemed to be surprised that dreams could
include talking. Yet, dreams remind me most of those flights of fantasy
when as a child we imagine conversations, scenarios, actions and we
create dramas. Sometimes if we did not like the ending, even the one
we made up, we simply said, "do-over" and fixed the ending to our
liking. While dreams do not exactly let us do that, we often edit our
dreams to our liking once we wake up. Hence, dreams create a space
that is less judgmental than our waking mind.

35

My dreams include the museum of my experience.

There is some evidence that dreaming assists part of the memory process called *consolidation.*[17] Some research asserts that dreams are responsible for making memories permanent by etching the experience on our cerebral cortex. For example, while doing brain surgery, surgeons notice that some specific memories have an exact location on the cortex. If they use an electrode to stimulate a particular spot on a person's brain, that spot leads to the recall of a specific event from their life with images and sounds, etc. Interestingly, each person's cortex seems to be cobbled together with their own pattern of memories so there is no exact cortical spot for everyone that may always elicit "memories of mother." Certain areas have primarily visual or auditory information, but we can only find a certain memory through trial and error. There are a couple of areas where the function of speech appears to be the same in all brains (e.g., Broca's area).

Some people frequently have dreams about the past, which might include buildings (e.g., high school), people (grade school friends), and even memories of otherwise forgotten events. The question that should be asked is, "How does this retrieved memory fit into my life at this exact moment?" We then look for parallel "play" in our current situation and the situation that played out in the dream. The dream can function like a museum by being a place where the past is not dead but is still being integrated into our existence. Thus, dreams can enrich our present being, aiding in the honoring of the past.

36

I often write down my dreams left-handed and in the dark

Not writing down any part of a dream and expecting to remember it in the morning is a bad idea. Dreams disappear quite quickly under any circumstances, but a few notes about a dream should get you 24 hours to recall so it can be written down. If you are serious about understanding your dreams, you will have to write them down daily. Note-taking often means rolling over while half asleep and trying to choose a few descriptive words about the major activities of the dream. This does mean sacrificing some of your sleep because you must be conscious enough to recall a dream. Upon waking and note-taking, there is the possibility that you may struggle with returning to sleep.

---

[17] Rasch, B., & Born, J. (2013). About sleep's role in memory. *Physiological Review, 93*(2), 681–766. doi:10.1152/physrev.00032.2012.

Yet, the payoff is big! You are creating a pathway to the unconscious and increasing the likelihood that an important dream will come through. Note-taking also keeps the flow of dreams coming.

Dreams will come more frequently if they are attended to the next day. In my book *An Artist's Thought Book,*[18] (I wrote: "Invite it! Welcome it! Enjoy it! Thank it! (repeat)." This means that when you do have a dream, you should "thank it" by writing it down. It is best to have your bedside table set up in the direction that favors your writing hand. I have found that writing down dreams half asleep with my left hand is not a good practice for reading the notes the next day. Getting the good side of the bed for writing down dreams may require negotiating with your partner!

37

The narration of the dream tends to set the nonlinear events into an order.

When answering "What was your dream about?" the dreamer typically resorts to a "factual" recounting of the dream: who, what, when, where and how. This is the typical sensibility of the waking mind. Here, a prominent action that happens later in a dream will be recounted as the main meaning of the dream. Because we have the desire to make sense of our dreams, we have a tendency to recount them as stories with a beginning, middle, and end. The ending of the story becomes the most important part because it seems to contain the moral. Dreams befuddle us because we try to seek closure, morals, and definitive truth.

Maybe a better question to ask is, "How did the dream unfold?" This question attempts to get us to assess the dream from a chronological perspective rather than from a "moral of the story" perspective that the previous question elicits. In general, dreams are metaphorical and not literal or factual. In other words, we will discover that dreams are more about the process than the content. Process means *how the message is described* rather than what the message is. I find that while writing down or narrating the dream, I often stumble upon the meaning in the words I choose to use in the description. A phrase like "I just caught up to my dad" can reveal the physical action of running to meet up with my father in the dream, but it also could reveal the psychological meaning

---

[18] Bargdill, R.W. (2014) *An artist's thought book: Intriguing thoughts about the artistic process* (2nd ed.). University Professors Press.

of feeling that I am finally measuring up to his expectations of me. Your descriptions are the meaning.

38

My dreams are not foolish.

There are numerous people who believe that dreams are nonsense. There is a theory (Hobson and McCarley[19]) that suggests dreams are simply neurons firing randomly that accidentally become conscious and then are made into a story by the narrative-loving brain. I jokingly call this the "screen saver" theory of dreaming—as if the brain is keeping itself minimally active by stimulating the cortex every 90 minutes or so during sleep. Both of these attitudes take a reductionist approach, explaining away the deep mystery of dreams by claiming they are foolish.

If you want to err on the side of caution, you should assume all dreams are very meaningful. It is better to assume that a dream is a message, a comment, a warning, or a prophecy rather than assume there is no meaning. Yes, there are dreams that appear mundane, and there seems to be no "earth-shaking" commentary to be pulled from them. However, even these are not necessarily "message-less" dreams. They might be suggesting you are in a period where you must just take care of business. You are doing the small things that have to be done to ensure that your world stays in a stable state. Therefore, even mundane dreams can be some form of kudos. Our lives cannot be in high gear all the time.

But the majority of dreams are related to the emotional energy of your life, and so the likelihood is that more times than not dreams will be more evocative.

39

One more thought is destructive to the memory of a dream.

Dreams are fragile. Without reinforcement, they can disappear the moment that you turn your attention to anything else. When you wake

---

[19] Hobson, J.A., & McCarley, R.W. (1977). The brain as a dream state generator: An activation-synthesis hypothesis of the dream process. *The American Journal of Psychiatry, 134*(12),1335–1348.

up and have a dream in your consciousness and your goal is to recall it in as much detail as possible, you cannot delay. Think of a dream as a fuse on a firecracker. The moment you become awake is the moment that the fuse is lit and starts to burn up. The fuse is the entirety of the dream, and the more other events, like our day's schedule, have a chance to come into our mind, the more we lose connection to the details of that dream.

Many dreams seem to have multiple scenes, as if they were a play. As you relive the dream in your memory immediately upon waking, you can often recall only the most recent material. At that point the dream may reveal there is more than just the ending. You might remember the middle parts and sometimes even all the way back to the beginning of the dream. The key to recall the maximum aspects of the dream is to make sure there is the ability to silently contemplate the dream. Noises, distractions, music, and "must-do agendas" are all things that can quickly erase a dream's deeper passages.

Many times in my dream journals I will start the excerpt with the statement that this is only the end of the dream, which was much longer, but I cannot remember. This is nothing to feel guilty about, but it is worth noting as a dream sleuth that you want to gather as much as the story as you possibly can before it vanishes forever.

40

The meaning of a dream is often the paradox of two opposite possibilities, such as falling and ascending.

Dreams can reveal several of our hang-ups, fears, and complexes. Dreams sometimes perplex us because there appear to be "double meanings" or paradoxes to how a dream can be interpreted. The ambiguity of dreams reveals a more psychological truth, which is that many of our problems are due to the attempt to avoid one action that ultimately leads us to a behavior in the exact opposite direction. Dreams see our confusion.

Psychologically speaking, it is not uncommon to see a client in therapy who suffers from a lack of self-esteem and wishes to live life with more confidence. After some digging, we find that the client is also terrified of becoming an arrogant individual who belittles everyone else. Most of the time, these clients have had an upbringing where a parent had this exact trait, and their deep desire is to avoid becoming that person. So as a defense the client resists arrogance by never becoming too confident. Doubt is a confidence destroyer. The client is not even aware that they are reacting against arrogance by producing inferiority.

Dreams sometimes show us these paradoxes, such as both being close to reaching the apex of a mountain and yet fearful of falling from that mountain to our death. The dream reveals the confidence and insecurity dynamic.

41

Is there any real difference between dream and memory?

A dream usually appears to be a novel experience. Even repetitive dreams are typically not exact in every detail. The overall quality and plot of the dream (manifest content) is the same, but some aspects of the retelling stray from the original. We experience dreams disappearing from memory quickly once we wake. I believe the sudden disappearance of dreams occur so they are not confused with reality. Those who frequently recall dreams probably have confused a dream scenario with a waking situation at least one time. I found myself in a shower at 3:00 am because I woke from a realistic dream in which I had overslept and missed the next day's important events; however, these events did not start until normal business hours. Hence, distinguishing our reality from dreams is significant.

Once a dream is noted in consciousness, spoken to another, or written down, it also then becomes a memory. It would be fascinating to investigate whether a dream is always remembered as a dream or whether it is absorbed through memory decay as an actual experience. Most of our dreams contain some fantastic qualities that may eliminate them from being confused with reality. Yet, there are other mundane dreams that occur that could be confused for real events. Movies like *Blade Runner* and *Inception* play with this idea that memories can be implanted into a person's mind, with the latter using the concept that dreams are a way to input ideas into the head of the dreamer.

42

Whenever I'm in a creative slump, I can get out of it
by reading some of my old dreams.

Dreams are creative acts. Art, music, theatrical plots, and lyrical works are all possible outcomes of writing down your dreams. When I find that my creative life is in a downturn, I find this can be reversed by reading through old dreams. Reviewing dreams that you have written down is like seeing the imagination in its free-form state.

The plots of the dreams themselves make good short stories. A song can be constructed based on the action of the dream. I once wrote a song in 20 minutes that followed the basic outline of the dream. Dreams can contain music inside them, often disguised as music of a known composer; but many times, the music is unique and not already invented, and thus that music is yours!

Another way to bust out of a creative slump is to "request" a dream from your unconscious that night. When you "set the intention" to receive an inspiring dream, you most likely will get a dream of some kind. You can also ask more specifically for a dream that tells a story for a song or play. Ask for what you want and see what comes up. If you request, you are likely to find that the dream in some way does give you something of value.

43

You can get everything you want to in your dreams. I was fifty but finally kissed the pretty girl from high school.

Freud was famous for saying that most dreams express a *wish fulfillment,*[20] meaning you are able to do things in your dreams that you cannot or would not dare do in waking life. In my younger years, I have often found this suggestion to be an overstatement. Some dreams can easily be seen as wish fulfillments, such as the one I mention, but certainly not every dream. Any dream that would be considered a nightmare would not be a wish fulfilled, unless we think that we secretly want to be punished for our unconscious desires. This is not that far-fetched since we clearly see people who, from our perspective, have a self-destructive pattern of behavior.

Freud's book on dream interpretation was written during his mid-life, and his observations may be due to the stage of development he was in at the time, so it does not necessarily apply to younger dreamers. Having reached mid-life, I have found that a number of my dreams *do* seem to be fulfilling a wish. I have played golf with Tiger Woods, I have been a backup singer for Bob Dylan, and got to kiss that girl from high

---

[20] Freud, S. (2010). *The interpretation of dreams.* (J. Strachey, Trans.). Basic Books (original work published 1900)

school that I did not have a chance with back then. I think this reflects this period in my life where I am successful enough that I am asking my unconscious mind what are some things that I would like to accomplish before my life winds down. Yet, I have twenty years of dreams recorded prior to this point in which less than 10% could be considered fulfilling wishes. So, our dreams change with our stages of life.

44

The more you think like dreams, the more you become an artist.

Dreams have a much more ambiguous and mysterious quality to them compared to our ordinary lives. Dreams do not lecture us. Very rarely do we have dreams in which the main feature is listening to a speaker just talk! Rather, dreams are visual, and when they want to convey a meaning, they do so with poignant action, dramatic scenery, intruding animals, and transcendent abilities. As Boss notes,[21] what is possible is greatly increased in dreams, and being able to entertain possibility is the foundation of being an artist.

One attitude that I see in a good number of people who claim that they are "not creative" is the habit of criticizing a project prior to even beginning it. One of the most important aspects of being an artist is to get the project started, and once it has begun one can troubleshoot as the problems arise. You will hear many people speak about staring at a blank canvas or sitting down at the typewriter looking at the empty page. People can get stuck wanting the first stroke of the brush or keyboard to be just perfect. The odds are that most great opening lines were not written first but were composed after the project was largely on its way or even in its final stages.

Dreams show us that they, too, can have a narrative that is moving in one direction and then they suddenly make a big shift. The dream-me does not even seem to care about the context, location, and people involved that have all changed in an instant. The dream-me just goes with the flow of the scenario.

45

Dreams make good song plots.

---

[21] Boss, M. (1957). *The Analysis of Dreams* (J. Pomerans, Trans.). Philosophical Library.

Since I have suggested this before, I would like to share a dream and the song that I wrote based on the dream. Here is the dream:

> A beautiful woman enters the establishment where I am a bartender. She is followed a few seconds later by a suspicious-looking guy. But the two don't sit together, so it doesn't seem to be related. She sits at a bar and he sits at a table. He is watching her. She flirts with me and waits around for me to get off work. The man is one of the last to leave before the bar closes. She comes back with me to my rustic log cabin. She spends the night. The next day, I'm getting ready to leave for work, and she gets picked up at my place by the suspicious guy who I now take to be her brother.
>
> As my shift nears its end, I hear fire truck sirens. I go out the bar's front door to see smoke in the general direction of my home. The dream ends as I arrive at my log cabin to see it was the source of the fire. I realize that I was set up by this crime duo.

Here are the song lyrics:

Auspicious Beginnings.[22]

It began with an auspicious beginning.
Of course, I was the innocent one.
Left in a burning log cabin,
And caught with my prints on the gun

I could tell they left in a hurry.
Zippo and smokes lay on the floor.
One gun thrown in the fireplace,
all my cash was gone from the drawer.

Chorus:

When you see the Stop signs in your life
And you've rolled through another one
and you hear the Sirens in your mind
But you still find yourself on the run

---

[22] Copyright Richard Bargdill.

But you don't know what you're running from.

No doubt I was guilty by association
when I heard the voice on the bullhorn.
And just like a rat in a corner
my thoughts lost their shape and their form.

Now I've done some things that were stupid
I've been drunk and high and been pissed
But in a sudden moment of enlightenment
I decided not to add to the list.

Chorus:

I wiped off the gun and the trigger.
I stamped out the fire with my foot.
I took a deep breath to just mellow
I fanned away some down-floating soot.

Outside I took my last breath of freedom
I knew the cops would treat me rough
With my face in the dirt, I took a kick for a smirk
Because I surrendered but I didn't give up.

46

*Dreams are like the wave particles of consciousness
while "reality" is the home of consciousness in matter form.*

The popular (and minimal) understanding of quantum physics by the lay person includes the idea that energy can operate either as a packet or as a wave. In addition, scientists cannot tell which way the energy is behaving in advance, and it requires some kind of observation of the situation in order to determine which of the two behaviors has occurred. Naturally, quantum physics can get taken out of context, with non-physicists claiming that "consciousness determines reality."

However, it is not unfeasible that dreams and reality are two forms of knowledge that should be considered more equal than they are. Our contemporary world (although changing now) has held a longstanding bias against dreams. Reason, rationality, and reality have been king, and science is seen as the great truth maker. Oddly, when science cannot explain something, the scientists simply dismiss the unexplainable as "non-sense." Profound coincidences (synchronicities) are "just" a coincidence, a prophetic dream is "just" a dream, and a bad vibe is "just" irrational. We have to start investigating, as Carl Jung suggested, the things that do not fit easily into our rational world. Jung suggested that we are so happy when conditions can account for 95% of phenomena that we simply throw out the last 5% as errors.[23] Science seems disinterested in whatever does not fit nicely into its box rather than focusing on it.

47

I know I wasn't dreaming because I felt the sun on my back.
Can you dream about how the sun feels?

The answer is yes. Every human experience that we can feel in waking life we seem to be able to feel in dreams. In fact, there are things we can feel in dreams that we cannot feel in real life (flying without machines). As Medard Boss suggests,[24] we seem to have extra levels of freedom in the dreaming world that make it an arena of expanded consciousness.

Some laboratory experiments in dreaming have shown that external stimuli that are experienced while dreaming are incorporated in the dream. Many people have experienced their beeping alarm clock integrated into a dream narrative (e.g., the reversing sound made by a large truck). In one such study, a hot iron was placed near the face of a person in REM sleep[25]; then the person was awakened. When asked what they were dreaming about the awake-me reported that they were crawling through a hot desert and dying of thirst. A flower placed under a sleeping person's nose has elicited a dream about walking in a garden.

In my own experience, I had an aesthetic chill (goosebumps due to beauty) inside a dream while I was personally charting these occurrences during my awake times. Since I was also charting the body location of where the chills took place (i.e., back torso, back of neck, etc.) this chill presented a conundrum on how to locate the chill on the body map! In any case, it is clear that the body is not completely isolated from the unconscious mind while dreaming.

---

[23] Jung, C. G. (1993). *Synchronicity: An acausal connecting principle*. Bollingen Foundation. (Original work published 1952)
[24] Boss, M. (1957). *The analysis of dreams* (J. Pomerans, Trans.). Philosophical Library.
[25] Van de Castle, R.L. (1994). *Our dreaming mind*. Ballantine Books.

48

*Jet lag can mean you don't have any dreams until you become adjusted
to the time differences is close to completing that when dreams return.*

We know there are some experiences that disrupt the dream cycle. One
of those things is jet lag, where traveling a great distance can cause
struggles to acclimate to different sleeping and dreaming habits.
Sometimes dream memory does cease until it can get back on track to
sleeping in this particular time zone. However, dreaming seems to be
necessary, and if the dreaming process is interrupted due to travel, it is
often "made-up" in the near future once sleep cycles are restored. This
is called the REM Rebound effect.[26].

This rebound effect means that in the days after the disruption or
lack of dreaming, there will be increased dreaming from typical 10-
minute, 15-minute, or 30-minute dreams to 45 minutes. The dream
time does not seem to completely make up the missed dreaming time,
but it does increase itself from normal. This reaffirms that dreaming
must be necessary for maintaining normal physiological functioning
(i.e., memory consolidation).

People in sleep laboratories who have been allowed to get normal
amounts of sleep but have been stopped from dreaming while sleeping,
report being irritable and unrefreshed. Thus, dreaming seems an
important aspect of the sleep cycle for maintaining the homeostasis of
good mental hygiene.

49

*Dreams are visits to parallel universes at unknown and unpredictable
times.*

Dreams can take you to various places in the universe. Most of my
dreams seem to be terrestrial, but I have had a few dreams off Earth,
including a visit to Mars. In that dream, there was no need for space
suits, and it was noticeable that "my team" was not among the first
humans to be here as the landscape was a junkyard of our predecessor's
equipment. I have had a few other off-Earth dreams, but many of our

---

[26] Dement, W. (1960). The effect of dream deprivation: The need for a certain amount of
dreaming each night is suggested by recent experiments. *Science, 131* (3415), 1705–1707.
doi:10.1126/science.131.3415.1705.

dreams allow us the ability to move through time. I have had a handful of "prophetic" dreams in which a scene from the future is first dreamt then experienced not too far into the future. This is often accompanied by a feeling of déjà vu; thus, there has been no benefit to seeing the future.

I have gone backward in time all the way to early Roman times; Jung has suggested this usually occurs as one descends down staircases, escalators or elevators. The descending moves you from your personal unconscious into a deeper level. He posited the existence of a "cultural unconscious," and then even further down a "collective unconscious."[27] These levels often will be signaled by a deterioration of the architecture and lack of technology. There will no longer be escalators but wooden or stone stairs. If wood, they will be creaking and fragile, while stone steps will be worn. The walls of these areas will often have cracks and roots growing through them, and a common feature (for me) is that water is dripping through the lower levels.

50

The day started by remembering a dream I lost yesterday.

When you cannot remember a dream, but you know you had one, there is not a great rate of successful retrieval. The best luck I have had is simply to set the intention to get the dream back. "I want to remember that dream!" or "Please give me a detail that might allow me to remember the dream." Occasionally, this will work (less than 5% of the time). The dream fragment will appear— almost like that person's name you've been trying to recall all day— meaning the dream detail will arrive when you are not trying to remember it! Usually, some other feature triggers a memory that is similar to an event that occurred in the dream. For example, if a can of soup appeared in the lost dream and then in waking life you stumble upon a real can of soup, there may be a flash of the dream in your memory. Rarely, does this magic-retrieval occur after more than one day.

Another method I have used to recover a morning dream is to lie still in bed, attempting to think about nothing at all—the meditator's goal— and see if the dream comes back after being immediately invited. This has worked for me two or three times, but it is surely not foolproof.

---

[27] Jung, C. G. 1959). The concept of the collective unconscious. *Collected Works* (Vol. 9.1). (Original work published 1936)

With the proper mental stillness, the detail will reemerge in a minute or two. But that is about as long as I can keep the thoughts at bay, and soon I start to think "this is not working," which typically indicates that I have lost the possibility of dream recovery. Of course, if the theme of the dream is really important, it most likely will manifest itself in a different dream soon.

51

The reason that dreams lurch forward is because
they are editing out the boring parts.

Dreams seem to be packing the action into a short period of time. Most dreams have little time to waste on the "fine details"; hence, there are lurches in continuity and setting. In other instances, there are flat out omissions of any logical sequence. In a way, dreams are what we hope life can be (most of the time), one action-filled event after another. The dream removes all the boring parts of life, and instead we get to move from point A to point B immediately.

If you looked at your life in the same way dreams do, your life would be sped up to an almost break-neck speed. There would be no time on airplanes or waiting around for activities. Blip! You're in France. The action of a dream has the same qualities of a movie where in 90 minutes you can experience the action of weeks, months, years, or decades. How many movies end with some kind of black screen announcing a "one year later" scene? Dreams do the same thing. They show that we cannot anticipate how an event happening today will ultimately influence us in the future. Anyone who has gone through big changes often finds themselves laughing when they look back on life a year after those changes. All the minutiae do not really matter as long as the fundamentals that you hold are in place. It will work out in the way that the foundation suggests.

52

You can live a pretty ordinary life and still have extraordinary
adventures in your dreams.

One of the great aspects of dreams is that for the most part the dream-me has a first-person account of the action. This means that dream feels real and to some degree can show you how experiences might occur.

Yet, when you describe a great and unique dream to another person, they will explain away the dream by stating: "Yes, but it was just a dream." This discounting comment can be quite off-putting to the dreamer: after all, it felt real.[28] You had all the general sensations that seem to fit with what the waking experience also would have produced. So, what does it matter that it happened in one's dreams rather than reality?

My dreams have given me opportunities I would never be able to experience. I have met and interacted with numerous celebrities and famous thinkers. I have traveled to foreign countries multiple times. I have sailed on the open sea. All these adventures seem to be similar to things that I have experienced, thought, or imagined on a smaller scale. In fact, dreams of this kind may be encouraging me to "dream bigger." Most dream events probably turn out to be better than they would be in reality since there were no expenses or planning involved! Dreams give us experiences that are beyond what we may ever have otherwise in our lives. Dreams are, therefore, *bonus experiences*!

53

Trying to remember a dream a day later is like trying
to capture vapor with a sieve.

I had a poem about this phenomenon that got published:

Etch and Sketch

My dreams are held
In my head
Like the pictures
In the sand
And when I wake
I must be careful
Not to shake
The sleep too hard
From my head

---

[28] Craig, E. (1987). The realness of dreams. In R.A. Russo (Ed.). *Dreams are wiser than men.* (pp.34-57). North Atlantic Books.

54

My mind ate my dream.

As much as we value "intelligence" in the West, we have recently begun to recognize that our rational minds have some negative qualities. Meditation and mindfulness practices have shown us that our minds are running nonstop like gangbusters all day long and sometimes deep into the night. This spin cycle can be extraordinarily taxing, especially when we have a sleepless night in which we spend our "resting time" obsessing over a future event. This event never goes exactly the same way as any of the hundreds of misdirected ways that we anticipated it would. Worry and foresight are not the same thing. Worry anticipates detrimental results, while foresight imagines possible obstacles that we can prepare to avoid.

The mind can take us on a wild goose chase from one imagined catastrophe to another. We can also experience this in the morning when we wake from a dream and suddenly something else pops into our mind because it is seen as the most important thing for the awake-me. It takes great discipline to wake up and pause immediately so you can assess whether or not you had a dream last night. Recording dreams is a habit to be established, and like most good habits it will take several weeks.

Mindfulness is training that allows us to let the scatter-brainedness of normal consciousness slide by us so that we are not chasing every squirrel that runs past us. If we can practice mindfulness when we wake up, we have a much better chance of remembering that dream.

55

My dreams pay no attention to the ordinary laws of time.

Dreams have *existential temporality* because the linearity of time dissolves, and the past present and future are often swirled together. Linear time means that we only experience the present moment; the past is behind us is unalterable, and now becomes an objective fact. The future is out in front of us, existing as an uncertain series of possibilities. These are supposedly discrete domains that cannot be mingled. The future cannot be accessed by the past or the present and does not influence the present. This form of time is not the type we see in dreams. Time in dreams is interactive.

The past and present are frequently blended together. We find ourselves with long-lost friends and even in bodies that are remarkably younger than our present ones. Sometimes our homes have aspects from our true historical past; but most likely there is something that is not quite right about the house we know to be our home at that time of our life. We can also interact with people from our past that we no longer have any contact with. This might be due to estrangement, distance, or even death. The past is not truly dead in dreams. We can make amends with it.

We can experience the future in our dreams, but it is difficult to see it that way since we do not know what will happen in our lives, even if it is shown to us in advance. It simply looks like just another dream situation that has an unreal feeling about it. The times I have had prophetic dreams, I remembered how strange an element in the dream was, and that element then occurred later.

56

Today is tomorrow's dream.

Previously, we have spoken about how often a dream can contain an element of the previous day's action. The events in the dream will not necessarily be "exact" repeats of the actual details. We have to broaden our horizons in order to see the similarities, as the dreams are more likely to make passing references, "loose associations," or interpolations. Most of the time, there are at least two degrees of separation from actual events and the way it plays out in a dream. An example of this might be: After watching a documentary about Woodstock and the "Summer of Love," in that night's dream, you find yourself in a crowded nightclub, which is not something that you typically do nowadays. Maybe in the dream you have a particularly good time.

While a nightclub is not Woodstock, there is a commonality—music, dancing, and interacting with others. In order to understand the dream, you can ask some questions about your experience the previous day. How did the Woodstock documentary affect you? Were you wishing that you were there (i.e., feel like you missed out)? Did you reminisce about the past in a positive way? Did something happen to your awake-me that day that also made you, let's say, feel like you missed out on someplace where you would have liked to have been. Since it has been a long time since you have listened and danced to live music, could this dream possibly be commenting that you need to return to music-based activities that you used to enjoy?

Chapter 3

Observations

57

Dreams are a smoothing over of cognition, a balancing out of the rigidness of perception.

Dreams are incredibly accepting! Very little awakens the dreamer suddenly. Typically, only perceived physical violence to the body or extreme psychological fear will draw the dream-me back to the conscious state of being the awake-me. The dream-me has extraordinary tolerance for novelty. The dream-me goes with the flow in a way that few people would respond during their waking hours. A person's criticality is all but eliminated in the dream world, as wild scenarios and seemingly impossible transitions are accepted as if they were everyday occurrences. The rational powers are severely weakened.

Waking perception is quite rigid in that when we do not know what something is, we are plagued by the question: What the heck is that? Dreams introduce numerous abnormalities that dream-me embraces with little skepticisms. There is no "paralysis through analysis," second guessing, or hesitation that our awake-me goes through when making a single decision. Our dream-me seems to be truly in the "here and now" of a very fluid situation.

Perhaps one of the great overreaching messages of dreams is how we could benefit from approaching situations with a little more openness and less judgment.

58

Give me a moment. I'm sketching a dream.

There are a few ideas, insights, and epiphanies that immediately register and become permanent in your memory. Once you see them, you never forget them. However, many valuable, yet less dramatic, mental notes are much less permanent and require immediate recording or sustained rote repetition to be recalled even a short time later. Dreams are frequently of this delicate nature.

Each of the "maxims" that appear at the top of the page and precede the elaboration are thoughts I have had about dreams over 30 years. A maxim is a short, pithy phrase or sentence that has a self-contained insight. When you find that you have had an insightful idea wandering through your head, it is a good idea to get that to a more permanent place. Almost any distraction can prevent that good idea from being permanently recorded. It is like typing something in a computer program but not saving it before you shut the computer down.

Everything temporary requires attention. Sketching out a dream, writing down an idea, elaborating an impression, and noting a possible invention are all ways of attending to the unconscious source. If you take these tidbits seriously and care for them—most people do not—they will continue coming to you. To the average person, a fleeting thought is nothing important. However, the recording of dreams is valuing unconscious material. Take note of your transmissions!

59

It's nice to know (if my dreams are any indication) that
Long-lost friends occasionally will get a visit from me.

True friendship in this world is a rare commodity. Friends do not have to be there for you by obligation, as one may expect a family member to be. Friends choose to be with us despite our flaws. They find ways to overlook them because our overall relationship with them is judged to be valuable enough to put up with our foibles. Sadly, many of our great friendships will come to an end for one reason or another. Sometimes we move away from our friends and communities to take jobs elsewhere. At other times, the relationship takes a negative turn because some incident is seen as a betrayal of integrity that the friendship cannot overcome.

Dreams often contain a core of forgiveness within them. Most of the times when there is a dream of an estranged friend, the estrangement part is left out. The friend appears in the dream as if nothing has occurred, and we are doing something together as the team we once were. The dream serves as a healing place that recognizes the beauty in the old friendship, reuniting us. This reunion is almost always positive in my experience, to the extent that I believe the dream aims to restore our faith in human friendship. The dream seems to encourage us to get over our pettiness and let bygones be bygones. In a way, dreams teach us that friendship is bigger and more important than the less significant reasons we became estranged in the first place.

60

What a wonderful life this is that at night we may be visited by a dream.

There are people who take certain medications that prevent all memories of dreams.[29] Meanwhile, the claim by others that they do not dream is, as we have previously stated, not entirely accurate. Most people are not attending to dreams on a regular basis and become interested in them only when a particularly disturbing or interesting dream arises. If any of these conditions apply to you, hopefully, this book will inspire you to consider establishing a deeper relationship with your dreams. I firmly believe that dreams are messages from yourself to yourself, but they can also serve numerous other purposes.

Dreams can be warnings, commentaries, prophecies, visitations, reunions, and suggestions, but they can also be pure entertainment and joy. Dreams can take you to places that you will never be able to go to in the physical realm. You can be with people who you would never have a chance to be with in real life, including famous and deceased individuals. In most cases, dreams are like a delightful puzzle for us to contemplate in the morning and throughout our day, much like a daily horoscope!

Sometimes when I stir near morning time, and I have not remembered a dream yet, I repeat my intention to get a dream before trying to go back down under. It almost feels like I am fishing for a dream. I know they are around here, but I just have not hooked one yet. What a delight it is to be visited by a dream!

---

[29] Tribl, G. G., Wetter, T. C., Schredl, M. (2013). Dreaming under antidepressants: A systematic review on evidence in depressive patients and healthy volunteers. *Sleep Medicine Reviews*, *17*(2), 133–142. doi:10.1016/j.smrv.2012.05.001.

61

Dreams are never about facts; they are about "maybes."
That's what makes them so disturbingly fascinating.

Dreams are hypothetical situations that even the dreamer could not have imagined in most cases. In waking life, a friend might ask us a hypothetical question, which is usually a moral dilemma that is rather scarce on details. It presents us with a scenario that has us in a moral bind. The forced choice between this or that is what allows us to sharpen our mental skills; at the same time, it reveals a bit about our character. Most of these situations ask us if we would do what is easiest or most pleasurable (for us) or if we will do what is the harder choice— be the bigger person and do what is right.

In dreams, we often are in the same position as the hypothetical situation. However, instead of our answer coming from our rational side, we get to see how our dream-me figures out the puzzle that our unconscious mind has put to us. Because rationality often includes what we think others want from us, we do not always answer hypothetical questions 100% honestly. We want people to respect us and, therefore, are more likely to give an answer that shows us in a positive light. The dream can present us with actions that we may be more likely to "actually do," despite being somewhat embarrassing for us. This accounts for how we find ourselves embarrassed by the actions of our dream-me. Dreams can, thus, be commenting to us that we talk a big game, but underneath all our bravado our character is not as strong as we suggest.

62

My dreams, fantasies, and phantasms are the spices that I add to the
food of experience, which makes my life a tasty dish.

If one was granted the ability to ask for good things in life prior to being inserted into a soul here on Earth, some of the typical requests could be wealth, fame, beauty, health, and family. Most folks probably would not give much attention to requesting a "vivid dream life" since they would not see that as adding an appreciable amount of quality to their lives. Yet, being a "vivid dreamer" has to go into the same category as a life of adventure, travel, deep and meaningful experiences, and spiritual evolution.

We have all heard that money cannot buy happiness. Most of us have seen people with "everything" who are not happy at all. Fame is fickle and can shift quicker than you can imagine. A wrong turn of events at the end of an illustrious career can lead to total erasure of a legacy (e.g., college football coaching icon Joe Paterno). As I wrote in 2006, all the "big" things in life that we wish for come with some serious warning stories:[30] Power corrupts, beauty fades. and trying to hold on to both can lead to despots and disfiguring plastic surgery disasters.

While nothing is completely without negative experiences, travel, dreams and spiritual experiences are things that you can carry with you that do not necessarily benefit you on the outside but do make the journey worthwhile. The benefit of dreams is that they are something most people can do daily, whereas traveling to foreign places is restricted to once or twice a year.

63

A dream is the mind's screen saver.

Hobson and McCarley have suggested that our dreams are basically random neural activity that accidentally becomes conscious.[31] The theory means the brain stays active, but also slows down since one's metabolism decreases. We see this decrease in the heart rate and breathing cycles, too. Remember, the brain can never be revived like the heart can. If a heart is stopped, we can use physical stimulation (CPR) and even electro-shock (defibrillators) to restart the heart. The brain is different. If it ceases to function (flat lines), it cannot be rejuvenated. While we can still live in a comatose state (i.e., brain-dead), we will never regain consciousness.

According to Hobson and McCarley, during sleep the brain slows down, which we can see in an EEG as N-REM stages two to four, with the third and fourth stages being called slow-wave sleep. Then after slow wave sleep, we experience Rapid Eye Movement (REM) sleep when most people would remember a dream if woken up. These researchers suggest that dreaming is a "systems check" that allows the sleeper a window to respond to any potential real-life threat, which is

---

[30] Bargdill, R. W. (2006). Fate and destiny: Some historical differences between the concepts. *Journal of Theoretical and Philosophical Psychology, 26*(1&2), 205–220). https://doi.org/10.1037/h0091275

[31] Hobson. J.A. (1990). Dreams and the brain. In S. Krippner (Ed.) *Dreamtime & Dreamwork: Decoding the language of the night.* (pp. 215–223). Tarcher/Putnam.

not possible during deep N-Rem sleep. In slow-wave sleep, people often do not wake to loud noises, and if awakened are completely groggy. Dreams, then, are meaningless brain activity meant to pull us out of deep sleep so that we might respond to a threat. The narrative aspect of dreaming is a byproduct of becoming conscious of any neural activity.

64

The beauty of a dream is not finding the exact meaning
but rather its vectors of meaning.

There are dreams that do end in Ah-ha moments when you know for sure that you have the right meaning for that dream. But these are pretty rare occurrences (less than 10% of time). A more likely occurrence is that you will discern several possible "vectors" of meaning in the dream. Dreams are more likely to take you to a place where there is a choice between three doors. Each one has some interesting features that could be the message of the dream, but none of these is speaking directly to the dreamer.

This "showcase of meanings" is the real beauty of dreaming. The dreamer can then explore the possibilities of each of the tunnels and look at the hints and markings on the wall. The dreamer may not be able to explore the cave of meaning too much at this particular time, but it is often enough to know that the space is there and that this can be the source of future dreams. Dreams often come in series. It is not uncommon for a particular character to show up in several dreams in a sequence. A different tunnel implies a variety of other meanings. For example, we may have a character from our ancient past (childhood) intermingling with a character from college. This dream can be sharing insights on each "level of development," which can be explored individually. But we can also see that this is a "longstanding" issue. The overall emotionality of the dream should connect to some psychological aspect that has concerned or benefited you throughout your life. That is the gift.

65

Dreams show that some knowledge is intuitive
and some genetic or platonic.

One of the mind-blowing aspects of Carl Jung's idea of the collective unconscious[32] is that somehow the knowledge and experiences of the past are not completely erased from contact for human beings. If we think about what "heredity" means, we seem to accept that our bodies are genetically influenced by previous generations of humans in our line. How tall we are, what our face looks like, and how susceptible we are to various diseases are qualities that we see as passed down by some information in our genes. Oddly, most of us do not seem to think anything related to our minds is passed down. Rather, we see ourselves as a tabula rasa (i.e., blank slate). This fits with our experience. Most people do not feel like they have lived previous lives; nor do they have access to the knowledge of unknown relatives.

The collective unconscious implies that the experiences and knowledge we acquire as humans also get stored somewhere and that the living have access to that information under certain circumstances. Dreams are one access point to our former experiences and knowledge. The idea that we can develop our intuitive powers and that they can guide us means there has to be wisdom already within the system. This takes us more in a Platonic direction. Plato believed that knowledge acquired during our lives was erased when we began a new life, but our thinking still flows down a similar logic path. Thus, dreams can provide the opportunities to develop intuitive wisdom.

66

Ever notice how few of your dreams contain snow?

While this might be easy to say for those of us who live in temperate climates, it is interesting to think about how often weather conditions occur in dreams. Many people concern themselves with the weather on a regular basis. Snow is a possibility where I live for about three months out of the year, and I have lived in places where snow is possible for up to six months a year. So, I might expect to see a little more snow in my dreams than I do. Rain does occur in my dreams once in a while, but I am not sure if I can recall any dreams where severe wind is part of the dream, other than possibly a hurricane-type disaster dream.

That means, for the most part, I have good weather in the dream, or the dream takes place, where weather conditions are not a feature of

---

[32] Jung, C. G. (1953). The structure of the unconscious. *Collected works* (Vol. 7; pp. 263–292). (Original published in 1916)

the dream. Some dream research called "Content Analysis" attempts to count the number of times particular incidents occur in dreams.[33] This type of research is often used in cross-cultural studies. It can be used to compare how often Western people dream of sex compared to the frequencies in Asian cultures. (Westerners dream of sex a lot more.) It certainly would be interesting to look at a year's worth of dreams and see how many mention the weather, and what percentage of these dreams include rain, snow, sleet, and pure sunshine. The lack of weather may indicate that dreams are concerned with the internal world and not the external one.

67

No one else has ever had the dreams I have had about love.

When I look at all the affection that has come my way in dreams, it certainly seems like the unconscious world does counterbalance what is happening in the waking world. Our waking life is frequently a place where compliments are rare, love appears to be elusive, and true community is all but nearly extinct. The dream world can be a very positive place compared to the desolate real world. I must say that I probably have a good dream-to-nightmare ratio of 30 to 1.

There is no doubt that our dreams can contain threats and anxiety, but dreams also have friendship, shared goals, and, quite frequently, sex (and love)! Dreams, being largely visual mediums, will often use sex as a visual representation of several positive emotions that include caring, affection, love, admiration, intellectual turn-ons, and reconciliation. We must consider all of these possibilities when sex is included in the action of dreams. Gone are the days when, with confidence, Freud said that "Sex means sex."[34]

In our waking lives, we may not have that many love affairs, even when we look back over a lifetime. In our dreams, we have numerous characters who we know to be our current lovers despite not looking at all like those people. Yet, these dream lovers can still teach us things about interacting with others. They can remind us that we have beautiful qualities even if our current partner does not see them. And

---

[33] Hill, C. S. (1966). *The content analysis of dreams.* Appleton Century Crofts.
[34] Freud, S. (1962). *Three essays on the theory of sexuality* (J. Strachey, Trans.). Basic Books.

in some cases they can remind us that we have some self-improvement work left undone.

68

I must shut out my dream world because I can't live
in two worlds at once this week.

Dreams can come in clusters, and there are times when you find yourself overwhelmed by the number of complex dreams that arrive on your doorstep. Also, anxiety can cause people to wake up more frequently and thus increase the likelihood of remembering dreams. When we already have so much on our plate, having dreams at night can seem like a burden. We may need to take a break from our dreams at night. Once again, we can set the intention to "have uninterrupted sleep."

As we have previously mentioned, dreams occur every night, and our memory of dreams can be enhanced by asking to recall them. The counter to that is also possible: asking not to remember them. We do not have to worry that we will "never recall" a dream again since we have tied our desire not to be awakened by our dreams to the current stress we are experiencing. Even if we forget to ask to remember our dreams once the stress has passed, we will eventually have a dream that comes through.

When we are ready, our unconscious will recognize that the stress has diminished and show us another dream. Even the "non-dreamer" is occasionally given dreams, whether nightmares or fantastic adventures, that break through the barrier and into consciousness. Dreams will get through, and once you have one, you can thank it and reiterate: "My dreams are important to me. I want to remember my dreams."

69

The more you think about a dream, the more
it will seem like a prophecy.

Déjà vu occurs when a novel situation is experienced as a repeating experience. Even though you know you have never been here or done that, you have this flash of feeling that you have. As I have aged (it seems that déjà vu is more common in youth), most of my déjà vu experiences have seemed to come as a result of dreaming something that turns out to be similar to something that I'm now experiencing.

My theory on déjà vu is that the experience of time is similar to the structure of our DNA. Thus, time is also a double helix; a double helix means there is a twisting ladder-like structure. Dreams can act as rungs, and certain dreams allow us to see forward into the future by crossing the rung of the ladder to a future time where our dream will take place. When we wake up, the dream of the future is really not that much stranger than an ordinary dream, so it typically does not stand out. However, when we experience the similar circumstances that the dream suggested, then we have the profound déjà vu experience. This typically requires that we remember the dream distinctly for some reason, and then experience that the dream was prophetic. I owe my interest in dreaming to a prophetic dream because that experience touched me so deeply that I started writing down my dreams. After all, I felt I could see the future. Yet, the déjà vu experience is so sudden that there is no time to act on the prophetic nature of the dream.

70

When you die, you don't disappear until you
no longer show up in anyone's dreams.

When deceased relatives show up in your dreams—sometimes called visitation dreams—we seldom experience in the dream that they are dead. Most dreams have the relative interacting in no way as a ghost or spirit but as a living being doing typical activities in line with the scenario in the dream. In other words, they are not dead to us in the dream.

Many ancient cultures took these visitations to be the main purpose of dreams[35]—to receive additional wisdom from one's deceased elders. Anything that the elders said directly in the dream or was generally implied was taken as advice that should not be ignored. Thus, the dreamer was strongly encouraged to follow the instructions precisely as described. After all, the dead relative had traveled a long way to deliver this message.

---

[35] Kilbourne, B. (1990). Ancient and native people's dreams. In S. Krippner (Ed.), *Dreamtime and dreamwork: Decoding the language of the nigh.* (pp.194–214). Tarcher/Putnam.

This gives us a little indication about what kind of aether the dream world is: Time, space, and embodiment are all fluid. We can probably understand the dream world as a place in between our waking world and the land of the spirits, where information and knowledge can still be passed back and forth between entities. So even after death one's spirit is still alive in those who dream, and maybe true death does not occur until no one dreams of you. Given the fact that dreams contain numerous individuals that are unfamiliar to the dreamer, it could be possible that the dream world is connected to the afterlife.

71

When powerful dreams occur, our friends will tell us
that "It was just a dream."

The Western world has stripped away all the power of intuition. Rationality has a nemesis, and that nemesis is intuition. Rationality is actively attempting to get all people to give up their connection to intuition, and one of the ways it does so is by calling intuition by the more derogatory name—irrational. When people are "too" emotional, they are considered irrational. When they believe that their dreams are powerful prophecies, they are irrational. When they see a coincidence between two events as being meaningful, they are surely irrational.

It would appear that when we are born, we have a much greater connection to the intuitive. Children say the darndest things since they have not been completely socialized by the institutions that will curb their creativity. Kids can see the truth much more clearly than those who have a better mastery of the language. Adults have been stripped of intuition by cultural preference for rationality, rote answers, and a "just-the-facts" mentality. Children seem to have more experiences of déjà vu, and appear to dream more than adults do. They often have a clearer ability to read people and pick up on their vibe. As children become exposed to more institutionalization, they lose this intuitive side and eventually, when they have little to no left, they are given their diploma and sent out into a largely dead world.

72

During the Covid pandemic, dreams were one of the only ways
that we could see each other in person.

In times of deprivation—such as we experienced with the COVID crisis, where we were socially isolated for an extended period—our dreams can be the conduit to our social relationships. Numerous people found that their dreams intensified during the pandemic, and they had higher dream recall. The memory of dreams during this period was aided by the fact that the dreams were experienced as being more intense.

Another advantage of dreaming during the crisis was that it was the only way to see friends that I used to hang out with regularly. I noticed I had numerous dreams that included encountering my friends whom I was yearning to be in contact with. These dreams acted as "wish fulfillment" by accommodating a conscious desire that aligns line with Freud's theory.[36]

In the 2001 movie *Atanarjuat: The Fast Runner*, we see a scene where a man needs to communicate with an older woman over long distances in a time before telephones. That night, the person appears in the distant woman's dream and reveals the emergency that requires immediate action. The female dreamer takes this dream as the sign it was intended to be. This may seem telepathic, but this may have been one of the evolutionary uses for dreams. It would seem that the man needed to communicate and set an intention to do so... Since there are no other means to communicate, that dream becomes a transmission to the other person.

73

Imagination, dreams, and reality embody the triple point of the mind. If you can find your destination in any of them, you have made it home.

Water typically exists in one of its three forms at one time. It can be fluid water, solid ice, or gaseous water vapor (steam). Differences in atmospheric pressure and temperature determine the state H_2O takes; we are very familiar with the idea that at a particular temperature, water will turn to ice or steam. Those specific temperatures can be changed a little if the atmospheric pressure changes. When you go to a higher elevation, the amount of time you have to cook food if you are boiling it increases. In a laboratory, researchers can get all three phases

---

[36] Freud, S. (2010). *The interpretation of dreams* (J. Strachey, Trans.). Basic Books. (original work published 1900)

of water to occur simultaneously; this is called the "triple point of water."

Déjà vu appears to be involved in the "triple point of the mind" since this is a place where dreams, imaginings, and memories can all be experienced simultaneously in our reality. The uncanny experience of déjà vu is like coming to crossroads where you recognize the location. Still, you experienced it from a different direction—like discovering you can get to the same place by taking a backroad you didn't know existed. At this point, we cannot determine if we dreamed it, imagined it, or experienced it. Recent studies suggest that at least 10% of our actions fall into "dream–reality confusion." We cannot tell if it was a dream, an imagination, or a real memory. Our own mind is like a group of friends who cannot agree on the exact details of a funny memory.

74

The dream world and the real world are tipping poles.
That's why everyone's dreams can be intense even if real life is not.

Jung had the overarching idea that dreams helped balance out our psyche. He called this *compensation*.[37] Even if we live a wild life while awake, we might have dreams at night that may be ordinary. This would benefit us by giving us some downtime at night to recover so that we could be "up and at 'em" in the morning. If we are wild in the daytime and even more wild at night, then we begin living a life of burning the candle at both ends. Without some rest, our exhaustion and burnout seem like it will only be a matter of time before we collapse.

On the other hand, if your waking world is somewhat predictable and there is not much that excites your routine during the day, you might have an adventure at night. This nighttime zest could be reinvigorating and put some spring in your step that your daily life can feed off. Hence, dreams can charge your battery in either case: providing a rest for an over-active soul or a creative boost for a person burdened with the mundane.

Compensation also extends to the masculine and feminine aspects of our personality. If our personalities exude too much machismo, then a female visitor will come to the male dreamer and display compassion,

---

[37] Jung, C. G. (1984). *Dream analysis: Notes of the seminar given in 1928–1930*. Princeton University.

kindness, and non-competitiveness. This female visitor is trying to get the dreamer to soften their stance.

75

Dreams and creativity insights are made of the same stuff.
This explains why they can both disappear quickly.

Invisible ink is something that is applied wet and apparently disappears to the naked eye. Someone who knows that there is, in fact, a message there and knows the method to retrieve it can take the blank piece of paper and restore the message. Many of our most creative ideas seem to be made of this same type of material.

Dreams, insights, pieces of poetry, and ideas for inventions are all lightning flashes of discovery. They seem so hot and bright that we tend to think (erroneously) that they will be burned into our memories forever. Yet, just like the idiom "a flash in the pan" suggests, the things that are so mentally combustible do not always get recorded in our long-term memory. Apparently, we do need to force ourselves to hit that *save* button. If we do not intentionally do so, it is likely we see the paper as blank and do not realize that there might be a message there for us.

Why are these particular items so difficult to recall? I think they all originate from the deep layers of the mind. Inventions are usually ideas that the thinker has been mulling over for many long hours and then suddenly burst into consciousness. It is similar to the name you cannot remember all day that suddenly returns when you are not thinking about it. They disappear because they still contain "unconscious residue," which makes them slippery to our conscious memory.

76

My dream wasn't that off! Dreams are better
at seeing the whole picture than the ego.

Dreams mean that your mind is still working at night, giving you a little "intellectual overtime." One of the more surprising things about dreaming is that the brain in REM sleep is just as active as the mind is when it is awake. Dream researchers who have people in the sleep laboratories[38] have to physically look at their participants to verify that they are dreaming and not awake because they cannot tell simply by looking at their EEGs. Meaning that the dreamer's brain patterns are identical to being awake. This also explains why it is possible sometimes to wake up in the morning and return to the very dream you were having.

To some extent, dreaming can create some extra time to consider a project. As we have mentioned, dreams frequently have been the assistant for numerous inventions and mathematical discoveries. Dreams do not use an abundance of logic to formulate an answer, and the answer is not likely to match up directly to the question stated on paper. But if you can learn to read between the lines, the dream can solve the big problems just as well as the ego.

The nimbleness of the dreamer's mind is the important part. Looking at the dream as a metaphor and being able to extrapolate or see the dream as a loose approximation allows the dream to connect the unconscious solution to the conscious problem. In other words, the overly rational person might be receiving solutions in their dreams but cannot see the dream as a helper.

77

Dreams are a test of your flexibility. They see if you are able to find a lesson even in the least rational places.

Generally, we think that a "closed" mind is a negative thing. But how do we really open a mind? Our minds are opened when we reconsider something we felt had a certain answer to. In the light of new evidence—even the firmest beliefs can be changed. We open our minds when we discover abilities that we thought were out of our reach; we open our minds when new possibilities are offered to us that might take us to new places. We open our minds whenever we try something new that we think we will not like only to discover that it is quite good. Education can open us to intellectual methods like reading, writing, and reflection. Oppressed people and their struggle for rights and safety open us as we can imagine our own families in a similar position. Travel opens our minds by showing us that there are other ways of living life. Others live life with less than we have but still with zest. Some do not live as if time

---

[38] Pace-Schott, E.F. (2011). REM sleep and dreaming. In B. N. Mallick; et al., (Eds.), *Rapid eye movement sleep: Regulation and function*. Cambridge University Press.

is money. Those in other places might not value dedication to work the same way you might.

Dreams are also part of this mind-opening process. They present numerous challenges to our awake-me that could have the more skeptical types willing to completely discount the possibility of some useful knowledge. But dreams are strange educators because they are experiences that show us that there is a different kind of knowledge that is not straightforward—that can enrich, educate, transform, and enliven the person who takes the time to study them.

78

Dreams are like having your own talk show, where
the guests are visions from different times of your life.

A good metaphor about the joyful aspect of dreams is that dreams are like a mashup of your own home movies with some creative input added. Dreams are some kind of message from yourself to yourself. And a dream is like a live-action talk show, where you get to interact with known and unknown guests in a skit-style variety show. The only differences are that the skits are not known to you in advance, as would be the case on TV, and the guests are not always who you think they are. You are often the host, the hero; but sometimes you are also a guest seen in the third person.

One of the exciting aspects of talk shows is that we get to meet a movie star outside the movie script's context. We could see the natural person, even though the show has a rough outline of what will occur (guests have approved the questions to be asked). It becomes most memorable when the guest steps beyond the typical expectations of "nice" conversation and says or does something outrageous or out of character from their typical typecast movie roles. This also happens to us in the dream scenario; thus, we can wake up embarrassed by our dream actions, just as many movie stars might regret their revealing comments on late-night shows.

Chapter 4

Meaning Interpretation

79

Every dream is a potential prophecy.

Prophecy is only helpful if you can benefit from the foreknowledge. Knowing the future is not useful if there is no wiggle room to benefit from it. Fate,[39] I have argued, means there is no freedom in the sequence of major events. Thus, you can only influence the minutiae of life. In most of my prophetic dreams, I did not see the dream as a real possibility until the event *reoccurred*. There was a clear foreseeing of the future event, but I did not have any other forewarnings that the dream of yore was going to come about now. The prophecy sneaks upon you as a déjà vu event rather than as something you could prepare for.

Most dreams have a sort of surreal quality to them, so you somehow become alerted that what you are seeing is a future reality and not just some other dream scenario. It could be that all dreams are prophecies, but this would require us to change our view of time to be multidimensional[40] and not moving in one direction. Dreams seem to suggest that we can go back into the past repeatedly and also view the future.

I once had a vision that each action a person takes could be seen moving infinitely in eight directions, as if this moment were surrounded by eight slight variations. If you looked sideways, the event went into an infinite regress of non-action, but most had a slight but not immediate effect of taking you on a slightly different path. Once you acted, that "bubble" was used or popped. Hence, if you were to time-

---

[39] Bargdill, R. W. (2006). Fate and destiny: Some historical differences between the concepts. *Journal of Theoretical and Philosophical Psychology*, 26(1&2), 205–220. https://doi.org/10.1037/h0091275

[40] Tolaas, J., & Ullman, M. (1979). Extrasensory communication in dreams. In B.B. Wolman (Ed.), *Handbook of dreams: Research, theories and applications*. (pp. 168–202). Van Nostrand Reinhold, Co.

travel backward, you could never do that action again but would have to do a similarly adjacent action.

80

*Whatever doesn't make sense in a dream is the place
to focus your attention.*

Use the paradox or ambiguity in a dream image as the *significant puzzle* of the dream. The paradox is the message that needs to be deciphered. A paradox means that two opposing truths seem to be true at the same time. What does not really make sense in an otherwise plotted and understandable dream is what needs to be reflected upon by waking consciousness. Working on the image means asking numerous times, "Could this mean this? Could this mean that?" Eventually, the awake-me usually has an Ah-ha moment when the answer is found.

For example, consider a dream that contains the image of a toilet in a stairwell. This is paradoxical because we do not think that toilets belong there. Here is how we might decipher this. What does a toilet represent: a place to relieve oneself and rid oneself of waste, a private space where one can take a break from others. What is a stairwell: a public space, a place to get to and from private residences or offices, a vertical transition area, a non-luxurious utility space. When you combine the two, you can get the clues: something that should be private is occurring in public. Imagine a couple fighting in public or something happening that should not be seen by others right there in plain sight. *The key is to ask yourself how this has happened to you in the last few days.* Dreams are reflective of recent experiences.

81

*Parents' dreams can mean you are looking for <u>advice,</u> while
grandparents' dreams mean looking for <u>wisdom.</u>*

Parents in our dreams can represent looking for direct advice. Parents have a tendency to tell their kids exactly what to do. Since parents are sometimes only 20 or 30 years older than their children, they have two methods of giving advice. One is that they imagine what they would want you to do in the situation, similar to telling a teen what a 30-year-old would do. This is usually outdated advice for the times that the teen is going through. Two, they give incredibly vague (but philosophical advice) like "just be yourself." This is pretty hard to digest for the teen who does not feel they have a clue as to who they are, let alone what they should do. Dreams of parents can suggest how they might handle the situation through their dream actions or comments. Maybe now that you are older, the advice might fit a bit better.

Grandparent advice is often closer to wisdom. In life, grandparents can recognize being too tough and too direct with their own children. So, they take a different approach with their grandchildren, relating via stories and letting parents be the strict ones. Grandparents will narrate a story about a similar situation, what they tried, and how it turned out. The story works better for the teen because the teen can pick what portion is relevant for their predicament. If you hear the teen's logic later, you will find it is surprising which part of the story they took as being inspirational. Grandparents can represent a *perspective change* rather than action.

82

Since my thoughts disappear almost as soon as I think them
I must be on the verge of thinking unconsciously: dream thinking.

In the scientific days of yore, you would hear about the "aether" or the "liminal spaces" that suggested there was a surrounding vapor that connected us to the universe. Much of that disappeared once we discovered that space is a vacuum without any such substance (e.g., Michelson–Morley experiment). However, sometimes when you experience *flow,* meaning you are completely in tune with your current task, then all your mental faculties are working in unison. Thus, your thinking also has access to everything in the aether.

These experiences of flow allow all the ideas floating in our heads to arrange themselves in an orderly manner so that we become able to instantaneously solve complex problems as if they were mere child's play. The solution appears so obvious that we realize we should have thought of it before; but, of course, rationality seems to keep the obvious answers locked behind large doors. Many inventions and artistic works have been said to be created like this—out of thin aether. Dreams have a similar quality in that impossible tasks or situations are solved in the easiest way. Dreams and creativity show us that if we fully concentrate and work diligently on a problem—both of these are required—and yet the solution does not arrive, then it is likely that the blockage is some assumption you have about how it must arrive.

Remove that assumption, and most likely the pieces of the puzzle suddenly fit.

83

*Compare your dreams to common **idioms** in your native language. Dreams are visual shortcuts just as idioms are linguistic shortcuts.*

I have found that putting the images into language is where the key to discovery happens. I believe that dreams are shorthand notes from yourself to yourself. They are comments, criticisms, suggestions, and directions that are disguised as common idioms in our language. Idioms are famous sayings[41] that contain some familiar message such as "That guy is a dirty rat" or "She's going downhill fast." The first idiom suggests a person is a liar or cheater; the second idiom suggests someone's behavior is getting out of control. Driving a car downhill without brakes is a common dream.

Dreams are visual experiences so they "show" rather than "tell." Dreams often attempt to convey their message in a short visual plot. There are not long dialogues in (my) dreams but near constant action. When we tell a dream to someone else, we *rearticulate* it. This is our opportunity to compare it to some common statement that we use often. I recently had a dream in which I was in a shower and someone handed me a plate. Then I wiped the plate on my behind and soiled the plate. I was puzzled by this ridiculous dream until I looked at the image. I realized the meaning using idioms: "I'm doing a shitty job of cleaning my plate." I had been telling people I was not taking on new projects (cleaning my plate), until I finished some old ones. Despite my claim, I have taken on several new projects anyway!

84

The dreamer must choose between infinite potential possibilities present in a dream and the one message that might move one's life forward. Look for the Ah-Ha.

---

[41] Bargdill, R. W. (2019). Dream idioms: Using chengyu, idioms and proverbs to interpret dreams. In L. Hoffman, M. Yang, F. J. Kaklauskas, A. Chan, & M. Mansilla. (Eds.), *Existential psychology East-West* (Vol. 1: Rev. & expanded ed.; pp. 259–264). University Professors Press.

Numerous dream researchers recognize that there are multiple meanings to dreams; some of these notable researchers include Karen Horney,[42] Freud, and Jung. In a sense, dreams can take us on a wild goose chase if we choose to try to track down all meanings behind the trap doors. This activity of following every thread of a dream is not very satisfying. When we have followed the major aspects without any sense of what the dream is trying to tell us, we can become frustrated. Certain dreams give us the sense that they are communicating something to us, like a puzzle or a quiz, and we feel the need to find the right answer.

The Ah-ha moment does not mean that you found a viable meaning for the dream; rather, it means you have found the meaning that needed to be heard at this moment. The Ah-ha is like the ringing of a bell; it immediately feels right and seems to be the answer to what the dream is communicating to us. Message dreams, where we do not receive the Ah-ha feeling are the ones that haunt us all day or even for several days. However, rest assured that if the dream itself has a message that it wants the dreamer to recognize, and yet the dreamer still has not, the dream will repeat itself. A repetitive dream is a second knock on the door of consciousness. These dreams say: *I'm really important and I'm going to come back until you figure me out.*

85

Each dream should contain one psychological insight.

Certain dream researchers (e.g., Hobson[43]) believe that dreams inherently contain no psychological insights. This radical stance is often called "biological reductionism" because these researchers see dreams as meaningless brain activity. This theory speculated that once the dreamer becomes conscious of the brain activity, their minds try to create a narrative out of the nonsense visual material. Thus, dreamers are really making a mountain out of a molehill. Hobson believes you can enjoy the dream, but it is not telling you anything. Other researchers, myself included, believe there are insights in all dreams. I want to challenge you to find at least one psychological insight in every dream you have—even the ones that seem the most mundane.

---

[42] Horney, K. (2020). Systematic self-analysis. In R. W. Bargdill (Ed.), *Living the good life: A psychological history* (2nd ed.; pp.95–108). Cognella.
[43] Hobson, J.A. (1988). *The dreaming brain.* Basic Books.

To do this, let us imagine casting the widest net possible rather than requiring that the dream use specific and easily identifiable references to our real life. This means we have to think more in terms of approximations, metaphors, and loose connections. Think of the investigators (police and journalists) who use those photograph boards placed on a wall, with some photos connected by strings to represent the web of connections. These boards (from the outside) seem to be worthless montages of random facts and tiny connections. However, recall how many times in the movies that the boards spark the insight that solves the crime.

86

Is it a talent to have a lot of dreams?

Having dreams is probably not a talent since we know that everyone dreams about four times a night if they get about 8 hours of sleep. Many people, however, do not report remembering any dreams at all. Other people recount one or two dreams a week. With a little practice and the intention of remembering your dreams, you can get to a much higher percentage of dream recall. If we estimate that we have 28 possible dreams a week, it would seem possible to retrieve at least one a day.

Asking to remember your dreams each night is a great way to retrieve your dreams. Talking about your dreams to other people and listening to other people's dreams regularly also shows that the dreaming process is of interest to you. This will likely increase your bounty of remembered dreams since intuitive acts, of which dreaming is one, appear to like conscious attention. It is very likely that you could retrieve one dream a night consistently if you take the time to record your dreams by taking some notes and then writing out a narrative. Do not get in the habit of judging the worthiness of the dream in the moment; just make your notes. Many times, the meaning of a dream is not discovered until the dream is written out and described to other people.

There are several nights where I have had three dreams. And writing out one's dreams is a commitment of time that must be added into one's morning routine. It is possible to remember all four dreaming sessions; I have done it a handful of times. In a general year, I write a narrative for about 300–320 dreams.

87

You have to rotate the significant symbol in the dream
until it matches the recency of the dreamer's experience.

The key to dream interpretation is to try to make some sense of what the dream means to you at the time of the dream. Even items from a TV show, movie, YouTube, or a TikTok clip can make it into your dreams at night. I remember on the very night I watched the movie *Gladiator*, with scenes of ancient Roman captives fighting lions in the Colosseum, I had a dream that included a lion. Big cats are not a typical feature of my dreams, so it was clearly a remnant of the movie I had just watched. A lion has many meanings: king of the jungle, a "pride" of lions, "sticking one's head in the lion's mouth," a fierce predator—once a majestic but now an endangered animal, the astrological sign Leo, the cowardly lion from the *Wizard of Oz*; and we might consider that *lion* sounds a lot like *lying*. This is what I mean by rotating the symbol. Freud called this "free association."[44]

Next, we look at our life for any experience that roughly matches the dream action. We attempt to draw some parallel through metaphor, allegory, simile, or idiom. The most promising place to look for parallels is in an emotional conflict you recently had. Most dreams use your emotions as action prompts. If everything is going great, you might "fly" in a dream; if you are being over-confident, you might fail. Emotional conflict will often appear as physical violence. Fear is generally fear, and you will be running from something. Phenomenological dream interpretation asks you to assess what is happening in the dream, regardless of the wild details.

88

The sad thing about last night's dream is that when I was
playing in the puddles, I still felt the reprimand
about wearing my good shoes, even though I was old.

Dreams are playful. We all can use a little more play in our lives. This dream reminds us that we value possessions more than we value experiences. Instead of giving ourselves over to the joy of jumping in puddles like a child, enjoying nature and the amazing fact that the very

---

[44] Jones, E. (1964). *The life and works of Sigmund Freud*. Penguin Books.

substance that we need to live falls directly out of the skies, we are trained to be practical, to protect our clothing instead of our sense of wonder. As a parent, I know it is important to teach our kids to take care of things, but that should not be at the expense of creativity.

Our schools are so focused on obedience to "critical" thinking that there is almost no room after elementary school for creativity at all. Sadly, thinking outside the box is valued so much in the real world, but we have very little training (while awake) on how to do that. Dreaming teaches a great deal about play: Things are not always what they seem, leaps in logic can land on solid ground, metaphors can convey deeper truths than the facts, the impossible is endangered once someone becomes motivated. Dreams are our lifeline to the well of creativity.

Finally, dreams can act as "morality tales" just like a novel or movie. They can ask us to question what is truly important in life. Our dream-me can behave in ways that are maybe better or worse than our awake-me. This can get us to contemplate how we should act in the future.

89

I have dreams in which I'm not at my house, but it's not my home.

Whenever one of my old homes appears in my dreams, there is something off about it. It is never just the way I remembered it. Even if it is a close representation of that house, there is a noticeable error. Sometimes there are places in the house that did not really exist, or doors and windows are on the wrong walls. For example, I lived in a house with a spiral staircase that stood at the front of the house. In the dream, this staircase appears, but now it is in the center of the house. This could be one way that dreams help us distinguish them from a memory.

It is also not uncommon for a home in a dream to contain a "secret room" that the dream-me discovers. So, a house can represent one's own psychological home—almost like your personality. A secret room is thus suggesting that there is a little more to you than you thought. You have more space to become who you are.

A house can also refer to an entire family. Recall the Poe story *The Fall of The House of Usher*. If you can say that something is not quite right about the house, it may indicate that the family situation is problematic. The "malfunction" is not the house but the family members.

Sometimes, the majority of a familiar house will be from one period of life (e.g., childhood) and yet some rooms are from a later time frame (college). This scenario might indicate that the larger issues of the dream, not just the layout of house, is a continuing issue that stretches in time; it started in childhood and continues to plague a person into young adulthood.

90

Maybe the biggest lesson we have to teach our child
is to cherish their dreams.

Children seem to have that moment when they are younger where they struggle to tell the difference between reality and dreams. Most parents have had their children wake them up with some kind of scary tale that the parents eventually discern to be a bad dream. After a few of these instances, the child's dream reports start to dwindle. Sadly, it might only be a few times a year that our children share their dreams with us. Once they are teens, with the increase in sexualized dreams they may be too embarrassed to tell us anything at all.

This is a shame since dreams can be such a vibrant addition to anyone's life. Dreams can reveal our desires, fears, insecurities, and also help us develop a rich inner life. Sharing our dreams with our family can help us understand symbols as well as develop our intuition.

The best thing we can do to foster an interest in dreams in our children is to talk about our own dreams in front of them. Putting a largely visual medium into words that allows another person to understand the action of the dream is another significant skill that can only be helpful to the developing child. If we can, it is best to share a dream maybe once a week on a certain day (e.g., at Sunday dinner). Since kids are more prone to embarrassment and projection, it is best when interpreting their dreams to say, "If this was my dream, to me it would mean…" This way the child does not feel defensive.

91

To play is to dream without judgment.

To dream is to play. To play is to dream while awake. Playing as a child is so beautiful because "reality" is not an obstacle. Adults have adopted their limitations and appear to hold a view that this "cannot" happen, which means the progress of the world is generally impossible. It is adults who maintain an attitude that giraffes cannot be blue and that stones cannot fly and all magic must be an illusion. Play is a place where anything can happen. Play opposes judgment. Judgement claims that something *is* a particular way, and it will always be that way. When we judge something, we take it from a possibility and try to make it a thing. By a thing, I mean an object or a non-changing entity. Play wants to preserve options; judgment is final. While judgment wants a rigid decision, play is fluid and flows toward a place with the most options.

Is play then just fantasy? No. Play is the imagination. Fantasy creates a world that is unreal. It is an invented world where the rules we live in are opened beyond their natural limits. Imagination means that with sustained effort possible changes might lead to a new reality with a lineage of foreseeable connections. Imagination is the property of a person who sees the possibility of something better. Often this person does not think they are the person most adapted to make the project happen. It is my contention that the person who sees the missing opportunity is, in fact, the person who is "called" to make that opportunity into a reality.

92

Sports dreams are full of lessons for the game of life.

I have a lot of dreams with sporting activities in them. This type of dream can speak to your "competitive" nature. If something has recently occurred outside the sporting arena that has you feeling competitive, this might be the event being referred to by the sports dream. Competitive feelings about any project might be the source of the sports metaphor: competition for status, affection, or psychological one-upmanship. Sports idioms are highly present in our culture: "playing not to lose," "team just going through the motions," "this group has the intangibles," "last minute score or goal" can be shown through sports metaphors in the dream.

As we get older, many of us stop playing sports competitively and, thus, may be missing the competitive juices that can flow when we are trying to prove ourselves in front of others. If life is getting kind of stale or feels like it lacks that spark and that you're underperforming, a sports dream might be indicating that you need reestablish your competitive edge. Going for a jog might be a great form of exercise but it is not necessarily as vivacious as being tied in a competitive game where the next point wins.

Sports are filled with numerous metaphors and idioms that I think are the true messages encoded in dreams. Thus, a sports metaphor might be the easiest way for the unconscious to communicate to the dreamer a message that would be most understood. So, what is the sports metaphor most exemplified in your sports dreams?

93

Your dreams are going to put you in some awkward situations.
Dreams have a lot of moving parts.

Dreams are the masters of hypothetical situations. They just do not tell you they are hypothetical. Instead, they just insert you into the situation and let your dream-me work its way out. Unfortunately, your dream-me does not know they are being watched as if the consciousness of your awake-self is some kind of surveillance system the dream-me does not know exists. Hence, the dream-me often acts in ways that displease the awake-me after the conscious mind has reviewed the hypothetical behavior and outcome. Dreams are a test of character.

We take personally the actions of our dream-me as being reflective of our awake-me, despite the fact that the settings are unique and the logic of dreams is clearly not the same as that of the waking world. Some criticism toward our dream-me is certainly because we perceive our dreams from the first-person perspective. Most of my dreams come from my POV—seeing out of my own eyes. Yet, other dreams have a third-person perspective, with the dream-me seen from a distance, as if consciousness is a video camera recording.

One detail worth noting is the estimated age of our dream-me. We have a tendency to expect our dream-me as always being our current age, when sometimes the character is being represented as a younger version of ourselves. A younger character suggests that the behavior we are experiencing now might have its origins in a less mature version of ourselves.

94

Sometimes you have to lose a new dream so that you take the time to
recover a more important older dream that you haven't recorded.

Sometimes you may recognize as you are waking up that you did indeed have two dreams that night. In this moment of remembering, you might consider assessing which of the two is the more important or significant and merits writing about at length. Please do not. Instead, jot some very brief notes about each dream as quickly as possible. If attention is turned to one of the two dreams, even for a short moment, the other dream is in danger of being lost completely.

Make a small note of one or two words rather than several sentences for the first dream. Same for the second dream—one, two, or three words. If you decide to write full sentences about the first dream, it means you risk losing the memory of the second. Once you get the gist of the dream, then you can continue to add a bit of detail on the first and then the second dream. I have lost the second dream many times after making extensive notes on the first dream. Dreams hang only in the ether of consciousness and, like vapor, disappear in seconds once attention is moved away from them.

With notes written down, your mind can reconstruct the first dream without fear of losing the entirety of the second. This may be surprising, but two or three minutes focusing on the one dream is enough to let the second one completely disappear.

95

Karmatic inversion: A dream can turn the tables and put you in the same psychological drama that just played out in real life, but on the opposite end of your actions.

The changing of fate is another aspect that can go undetected in a dream without close attention. Some actions you do to another person in your waking life, can then happen to you in a dream. In other words, your dream gives you a taste of your own medicine. If the damage can be undone, you can still take corrective action. A dream can make you change your mind.

I realized this when in waking life I was asked by a kindly stranger to look over some of their poems. I had previously not had much success as a poem mentor, so I politely declined. That night I dreamt that I had crash-landed my spaceship. I needed help to get back to the mothership. I saw a man and asked him to help. But he refused, suggesting he did not know how to get to the exact location. I needed to be at the mothership during the solstice—a mere two days away—or I would be stranded on the planet forever since my rescue would be aborted. Only after pleading with the male character, did he agree; still, he would only take me halfway, where I would hopefully meet up with some nomads who would take me to my destination. Twice lost on that journey, I doubted the quality of the man's help, but we did make it to the hand-off spot on time. The dream instructed me to help any person, even if my assistance was not that helpful. The dream had put me in the same position I had put the poet.

96

Death of your dream-me just returns you to home base.

Freud felt that dream material was not supposed to be remembered.[45] He also felt that sleep was essential to humans' well-being. Dreams often disturb sleep (e.g., nightmares), and when this happens it is a failure of the unconscious to keep the person asleep. At the same time, dreams help us to release some of the disturbing material that was repressed within the unconscious. This concept of displacement means that we transfer negative psychological energy to our dream-me, who largely carries out actions that the awake-me wants to do but cannot consciously acknowledge. For Freud, human beings would eventually snap or have a nervous breakdown without releasing some of their negative energy.

Dying, or being about to die, in a dream usually results in an automatic return to consciousness of the previously asleep dreamer. Most death dreams have to do with bodily harm: falling, crashing, being shot, etc. However, in my experience, near misses do not always bring about conscious awakening. In a number of dreams I have had, I could have easily been physically injured, but the dangerous actions did not wake me and the dream sort of miraculously continued on. This means that it is not always fear that awakens us as much as the fear of loss of embodiment. For me, a side puzzle is understanding how the dreamer returns to the same sleeping body since dreams can be seen in the third person. In astral projection, people have suggested that the body and soul are attached by a thread-like cord.

97

My uncle has appeared so often in my dreams recently that I'm wondering what he is here to tell me.

---

[45] Rycroft, C. (1995) *A critical dictionary of psychoanalysis.* Penguin Books.

The term *archetype*[46] can be applied to figures that repeatedly appear in your dreams. Jung used the term to suggest that there are a few types of general figures that appear in so many cultures that they are extremely common. Some examples of archetypes include the hero who does what cannot be done, the wise one who helps others find the right way, the child prodigy who seems to have extraordinary talent, the generous mother who takes care of her own and other children.

There are characters that disproportionately appear at a high rate in your dreams. I use the phenomenological method[47] of dream interpretation that asks "what" type of person were they, meaning what were their outstanding personality traits? Another question phenomenology concentrates on is "how" does the person generally carry themselves? Phenomenology concentrates on *what something is* and *how it shows itself*. So, characters who frequently appear probably represent a personal archetype rather than a "real person."

One of my uncles died suddenly at age 53 of a heart attack. He has been appearing frequently in my dreams as I approach my 53rd year. The "what" and "how" of my uncle suggests to me the following warnings: I have to take better care of my physical body, including cutting some personal habits shared by both me and my uncle. I have to reduce conflict in my personal relationships and recognize that my time is limited. Or I could meet the same fate as my uncle if I do not choose to do things differently.

98

Dreams that repeat in theme—but not in scene—
are your core issue: "I'm late; I have to do this but can't do it."

Any repetitive dream is worth your attention; you are being told something over and over. This is like someone knocking on your door a second time who does not seem to believe you are not home. Some dreams repeat themselves almost exactly in sequence, and that usually gets the dreamer's attention. Here, the dream receives the attention it wants: a conversation or contemplation about it. Other dreams repeat in theme, not scene, meaning the overall emotional theme is the same

---

[46] Knox, Jean (2003). *Archetype, attachment, analysis: Jungian psychology and the emergent mind.* Brunner-Routledge.
[47] Craig, P. E. (1990) An existential approach to dreamwork. In S. Krippner (Ed.), *Dreamtime and dreamwork: Decoding the language of the night.* (pp. 69–77). Tarcher/Putnam.

although the images are different. These might include "I do not have what I need to leave for some event," "I have shown up only to have missed the event," "I am here but physically naked at the event," or "I am completely confused about what to do."

People may overlook the key word in the dream: I am "late," I have "missed," I am "naked" or "confused." If I am back in my teens and the setting is that I am in high school, the message "I'm late" might concern not achieving what you wanted to by now, passed on a golden opportunity, or took too long to decide. It even could indicate pregnancy (the great late). The message in "I've missed" could mean longing for an activity rather than the more literal "did not attend some activity." Jung thought that naked dreams were about feeling psychologically naked or revealing too much information (showed one's hand). Confusion could be life confusion as in not knowing what to do next. Always consider the multiple meanings of a key dream word.

99

The only time you may be a "whole person"
is when you are your dream character.

Our dream-me seems to think differently than our awake-me, so maybe our dream character is not exactly us, but rather a doppelgänger. One of the fascinating parts of dreams is that there seems to be a complete lack of insight into the thinking that is going on inside the "mind" of the dream-me. Action happens without the internal monologue that is usually available to the awake-me. Is this what it really means to feel *whole?* To genuinely live in the present moment? The awake-me is always fractured, confused, and hesitant, and life seems hard to figure out. The awake-me is prone to second-guessing, ambivalence, and is preoccupied by ambiguity. None of this seems to be in play with the dream-me. There is no cognitive disclosure when dreaming, but it immediately turns on once the dream is over. We tend to second guess our dream-me's actions.

The dream-me seems to be a raw character that does not think his way through a situation but is constantly in motion. This might be what an "intuitive version" of ourselves acts like. Jung called the wholeness process *individuation*.[48] Seldom, if ever, does my dream-me seem to be

---

[48] Jung, C.G. (1974). *Dreams* (R.F.C. Hall, Trans.; pp. 288–289). Princeton University Press. (Original work published 1909)

crippled by doubt or anxiety or frustration. Even in dreams where there are extraordinarily frustrating circumstances, the dream-me keeps trying to find a way out and keeps fighting through the scenario. It is only when I wake up that the awake-me judges the dream as another "frustration" dream. The dream-me simply exhibits pure resilience.

100

Relationship inversions: Dreams of your parents can be commenting on your actions toward your own child by having your parents do something to you.

Dreams can exhibit "role reversals." You can dream that you are receiving treatment from a parent when in fact you are exhibiting behavior toward your child. In other words, the dream is doing unto you what you have done to others. For example, in waking life I had an argument with my son where I acted a little heavy-handed, resulting in one of those "because I said so" moments. Later that night, I had a dream that reversed the roles, although the scenario was a little different. In this case, the authority figure was not me, but my father and I was now the teenager. When he acted toward me the same way I had toward my son, the action did not seem as righteous. Dreams can make comments on our behavior. The message of this dream was clear: You would not have liked to be treated like this when you were a young adult, yet you did this exact thing to your teenager.

I became convinced about the realness of these relationship inversions from another dream that involved me and my father. On the previous day, I had some unpleasant interactions with my children. That night, I dreamed that my dad came home from work in a foul mood. My mother was there, and she was ready to tell my dad about my misbehavior. As my dad stomped into the room, I was right in his way, and instead of walking around me, he walked right through me as if he was a ghost. I got the message: I was him.

101

Accomplishment inversions: famous people might appear in your dreams as a form of encouragement.

Certain sports, like baseball, contain life wisdom such as "keep your eye on the ball" and "three strikes & you're out." This wisdom can apply to life by telling us we need to focus on what we are doing in the moment or that you only have a certain number of attempts to get something right. Team sports might be relevant to how our family or co-workers are working together, especially if one of our family members is on our dream sports team. Individual sports, like golf, might be commenting that you feel your life situation is all on your shoulders and that you are not getting any help figuring out this game. These dreams might be encouraging us to be more "playful" in our approach to living by commenting that we are being too serious.

Sports dreams can contribute to "accomplishment inversions." Like karmatic and relationship inversions, accomplishment inversions can provide opportunities to engage with athletes, artists, or celebrities that you would unlikely ever get a chance to meet, let alone engage with in their area of expertise. In dreams, I have played with famous golfers like Tiger Woods and Phil Michelson. In these dreams I have not embarrassed myself while golfing, although in real life I am a hack golfer. My take is that the dream is showing me that there's some activity (not golf) that I am being encouraged to stick with. These dreams are telling me that I'm making progress, and while true success has not come yet, "keep doing what you are doing."

102

Western Assault on Spirit:

Emotion is being irrational
Dreams are not a message but "only a dream."
Synchronicity is just a coincidence.
Art is useless.
Intuition is baseless subjectivity

The phenomenological method is a tool for investigating "lived experiences." This means the method is interested in *what* has happened to you and *how* you have made sense of that experience (or phenomenon). In natural science (mainstream) circles, there is an emphasis on "objectivity," which suggests that truth requires a stance that is free of values—an approach that is not influenced by interpretation or opinion. Paradoxically, the first step of most scientific endeavors begins with an "educated guess." This means that most projects have some subjective skin in the game. Yet, natural science views any subjectivity as mere opinion, and the interpretation of the researcher is deemed unworthy of scientific inclusion. Oddly, scientific papers end with Results, Discussion, and Conclusion sections, all of which require interpretation.

This rationality-only bias has left us with a culture that does not appreciate our lived experiences. If something is meaningful to you, that should be an important factor to our educated friends.. They tend to discount that meaning by saying it was "just" a dream, opinion, or coincidence. I believe we should see these as deep, meaningful events.

103

Some people have dreams of thriving in jail.

Dreams can often offer us a morality tale of a paradox to consider:[49] Something that seems impossible is occurring—thriving in jail. If we think about this imagery as an "approximation of our current situation," then it may fit our situation a little better. Here, the dream idiom might be suggesting that you are "making the best of the bad situation." It could also mean that under a very tightly structured environment you really have the chance to blossom. For example, people who budget money and balance their checkbook for the first time often discover that they have been spending an absurd amount of money on a daily luxury item (coffee to go). Once they recognize and change this, there is more money to go around. A restriction here leads to a surplus over there.

A dream of thriving in jail might also suggests that one might need to greatly simplify one's life. Everything in jail is done on a schedule: waking up, eating, exercising, and sleeping are activities that are all regimented and habitual. Establishing good habits is very difficult for most people, and "jail" is a place that structures our life for us. Jail restricts our choices and makes time for us to reflect on our actions. Time becomes something that we need to fill. Many political prisoners have used their time in jail to write memoirs, political treatises, and impressive works of art. Hence, a dream about jail might be asking you to consider a project that you have been putting off—something that takes time, commitment, and daily work that you might not have in your busy day-to-day life.

---

[49] Rossi, E.L (1985). *Dreams and the growth of personality: Expanding awareness in psychotherapy* (2nd ed.). Brunner/Mazel.

104

The key to dream interpretation is to verbalize the dream images
and evaluate the verbalization for metaphors relating
to one's psychological situation.

One of the keys to unlocking the meaning of dreams is to listen to yourself as you tell the dream to someone else. You should attempt to hear any key words or phrases that you naturally use. Instead of choosing your words wisely, it is best to just share the dream as you would in normal conversation. But also listen for any interesting turns of phrase, any emotion words and possibly idiomatic expressions. Idioms are common statements in your language that work as colorful shortcuts, such as "The cat got your tongue?" This idiom is used for a person who is generally talkative but is surprisingly silent at the moment. The dream idiom theory suggests that dreams use these expressions to communicate messages to the dreamer. Hence, a dream is a visual shortcut that uses idiomatic phrases. Imagine a cat that scratches or paws at the dreamer's mouth. The dream message would be clear: You are being too quiet now.

The individual words that you choose to describe the situation can also have multiple meanings. Dreams are like a game of charades; they can only communicate in images, so they have to show you the message in the most visual way possible. That might mean putting two images together or using a visual image that is a rough equivalent. Sex can mean attraction, approval, arousal, intellectual stimulation, care for, etc. Sex might be used as shortcut imagery because the other concepts require more complex nuances that the dream cannot convey.

Chapter 5

Theories about Dreams

105

Dreams use a physical action to represent a psychological intention.

One of Freud's great contributions to psychology was his observation that physical ailments could be the symptom of a bigger psychological issue.[50] It was not uncommon for Catholic school children to be told that if they masturbated that they would "go blind." Lo and behold, Freud started to see hysterical blindness, which meant that the patient would enter a hospital with blindness symptoms, but those symptoms would disappear in a few days. Since genuine blindness does not disappear at all, Freud understood that the ailment was not physical but rather psychological.

Dreams will also show us numerous physical ailments that are not real-life challenges, but we must take care to investigate how they might be metaphors or indicators of a psychological situation. I have already discussed how pregnancy does not necessarily mean to be with child but can mean something is growing within you, like a project or a new way of being. Death, too, is not about dying. It can mean that something—a relationship, a project, a job or a time of life—is coming to an end. Dreams in a desert can be speaking not to the barrenness of physical surroundings but of our existence.

I once had a dream where a current girlfriend of mine in real life came into my room. She shot me in the leg, but it was clear she was shooting to kill. While I did not ever see her as a violent type, I eventually understood that the relationship itself was "killing me." After the dream, we soon broke up.

---

[50] Freud, S., & Breuer, J. (1955). *Studies on hysteria* (Standard ed. Vol.2; J. Strachey, Trans.). Hogarth Press. (Original published 1895)

106

If your unconscious mind was trying to tell your conscious mind
something, would the dream-you listen?

It is my contention that dreams are messages from you to yourself. I suggest that dreams can serve as warnings, commentaries, prophecies, reproaches, morality tales, genuine-reveals, hypothetical situations, and even comical relief (i.e., nightmirth): (1) Warning dreams might show you in situations where the action is out of control, but the real implication is that your behavior is reckless. (2) Commentary dreams can often be repetitive-style dreams at least in an emotional context (i.e., not repetitive in exact details). Emotions like frustration, confusion, being unable to move freely, or inability to exit a situation (i.e., leave for work) can be themes. (3) Reproach dreams seem to reprimand your dream-me by putting you in situations that you have just put others in. These dreams often ask you to correct your previous day's behavior. (4) Prophecy dreams can show you some aspect of the unknown future, usually without enough context so that you can anticipate its arrival. (5) Genuine reveals are dreams that show deeply felt but possibly unacknowledged yearnings; they show you what you "really, really" want, which is beyond money and power. (6) Morality tale dreams violate some strongly held belief in waking life. (7) Nightmirth results from humorous dreams about living this human life. (8) Hypothetical dreams (most dreams) highlight new situations that we must now consider.

In short, I think dreams could be some kind of training, maybe even "soul school," where we are being prepared for the next phase of our existence.

107

It is no surprise that a creative insight can come to a person
in a dream when our confined mind is removed from linearity
and moves into multidimensional time.

Dreams provide one of two problem-solving zones.[51] First, rational processes allow us to contemplate the pros and cons of the action. We anticipate future consequences of the decision by "projecting possibilities forward" on how things might turn out. In this case, if we see that the negative consequences seem more probable than the positive, we generally stay away from the action—unless, of course, the slim possibility of success is too enticing. In a sense we are all gambling with our future.

The second form of problem solving is the intuitive approach. In this case, there are less "calculations," and we make decisions based on our gut feeling. The information is more of a hunch that does not speak of a well-formulated series of "yays and nays" but comes from a more hidden source. Modern life has preferred rational methods because the reasoning can be checked afterward. This does not mean that the rationale is any more successful, only that you have a paper trail of what went into the decision. The intuitive seems more magical because the decision comes out of thin air (at least that is how the rational side will see it). Sometimes people think of the intuitive as the "back burner of the mind" and rationality as the front burner. When using the front burner, you are watching and paying attention to every detail, whereas on the back burner, things simmer and meld together—where flavor happens!

108

Post Dream Rationality: Trying to make sense of insignificant aspects of a half-forgotten dream.

The rational mind is the only place where aspects can be "insignificant." That is because the rational mind judges what it sees and sorts it. Rationality likes to cut the picture down into a small focal point and disregard any background. This is similar to taking a photograph where all the context is removed and the only figure exists. Then this figure can be categorized. In a dream everything can be important. Even if we only remember one aspect of the dream, we can spend some time concentrating on how that aspect relates to our life.

---

[51] Delaney, G. (1990) Personal and professional problem solving in dreams. In S. Krippner (Ed.), *Dreamtime and dreamwork: Decoding the language of the night.* (pp. 93–100). Tarcher/Putnam.

If the dream presents us with something puzzling, then any untangling that we do could be time well spent. Simply asking "What could this mean?" is an expansive exercise. Consciousness needs space. Rationality is a constrictor—very necessary at times but also confining to the playful imagination that often makes our lives joyful. Allowing the dream image to mean something other than it is, frees yourself to find crevices of possibility that can give you guidance. For example, a dreamer talked about a squirrel inside his house attacking him when he was trying to let the animal out. In waking life there are plenty of squirrels around his house, but we came to suspect the squirrel represented his wife because they had a squabble the night before. The dream reminded me of the idiom "a cornered rat will attack" since the dreamer reported that his wife was angry that she had to do something unexpected for her husband.

109

Secondary revision sometimes shows us more
about ourselves than the dream itself does.

Secondary revision[52] is a phrase that Freud used to describe one of two situations: first, a report of a dream where details are initially forgotten and then later emerge. Freud felt that the fact that these details were not initially included in the dream-telling meant that they were more deeply unconscious than the previously revealed content and thus were doubly important for examining the meaning of the dream. Oftentimes when retelling a dream, certain parts are suddenly recalled that should be given extra attention, scrutiny, and weight.

Second are the revisions that came after the dreamer became awake. Many times, immediately after waking the dreamer wants to modify the dream's ending. They want to change the ending to fit what they want the reality to be rather than the dream's unconscious trajectory. I am not as excited about lucid dreaming as others are because once we can control the dream it is no longer an unconscious message. It is simply a conscious edit.

It is important to consider any type of secondary revision because we need to be open to what the dream was attempting to tell us and not just accept what we want to hear. If something is more repressed than

---

[52] Freud, S. (1953). *On dreams* (J. Strachey, Trans.). W.W. Norton. (Original work published 1901)

other things, we should at least consider why this aspect may have been forgotten. If we are altering the script later, we must ask ourselves: What was so disturbing about the original dream that makes us want to change it? What does this say about me?

110

It's bad when you feel ashamed of something
you didn't do in your dream.

Dreams often put us in moral situations that may seem foreign to us. Many times in our dreams, we engage in actions that violate our waking values (i.e., sex with forbidden partners, even though we cannot take "sex" as a literal action). But dreams can also show us that we are *not* as willing to engage in real-world actions to the extent that we believe we might be. A young lady dreams she agrees to get onto the back of a dirt bike simply because a man invites her to do so. She not only enjoys the wild ride but eventually encourages him to jump some mounds of dirt. Her awake-me claims she would never do this, but the dream-me sure had a good time. Such a dream may get us to question our resolve and moral commitment to the non-actions. Dreams suggest that a young person needs to take a few more risks in life in order to maintain some life vitality.

People who have performed courageous acts often report that their "selfless" act was spurred on because they had previously experienced a deep feeling of shame due to not acting with courage when a previous opportunity had presented itself. They felt that they were a coward in that moment and since that experience have resolved to act differently the next time such a situation appeared. Imagine if a dream is somehow preparing us for future actions by putting our dream-me in a situation that, once awake, we find our behavior passive.

111

Can your dreams be bigger than your sense of self?

The answer here is a definitive yes! Experiences like seeing oneself in the third person remind us of "near death experience" descriptions in which the person witnesses the entire room from a vantage point that allows them to see much more of the operating room than their body position would allow (even if they were conscious). Dreams can give us that "remote viewing" perspective that sees our dream-me in the third person. Dreams have been known to be prophetic[53] and see into the future, and that is not an ordinary skill that the average person has.

The unusual temporality (experience of time) is another aspect of dreams that makes them seem to be in touch with a larger unconsciousness. Time does not appear to be linear in dreams. Events do not seem to happen in order, and even if we can put them in order when we tell our dream to others, we have a sense that they did not exactly happen like that. It is our nature to tell a story in a particular way, so that's the best we can do. In our dreams, we seem to be able to be anywhere in our personal time sequence of events and memories going back to childhood all the way to our future selves. We seem to have access to times that precede us, such as ancient dreams of Rome. We have opportunities to travel into outer space and even land on other planets. According to Jung's idea of the collective unconscious, we may during certain dreams have the ability to be anywhere in human time. This is why I sometimes say: dreaming is soul school.

112

Humans learn to think deeply by trying to interpret their dreams.

Dreams want to tell us a secret. But the secret is in a language that is the equivalent of "broken English." We can somewhat recognize the words but do not completely understand the meaning immediately. After we spend some time within the dream, we get better at hearing the cadence and can gather the gist of what is being intended. The dream is a mystery that we have to spend some time thinking about to break the coded message into some useful knowledge. Those who see the dream as nonsense are spared the task of searching for meaning but are also robbed of the chance of finding wisdom.

The secret that the dream tells us is that there is more than mere appearance. We have to be open and expand our minds so that our insights come. Dreams fall into the linguistic realm of metaphor, simile, homophones, off rhyme, connotation, double entendre, and symbol. A dream is like a great film; there are multiple layers of meaning. Each time we consider a dream, our ability to see life as awe inspiring increases over how we saw it before.

---

[53] Jaffe, A. (1999). *An archetypal approach to death dreams and ghosts*. Daimon Verlag.

We have to adopt a less serious approach to our dreams than we hold in waking life. We cannot address a dream like we know it all; instead we should approach it with an attitude of *let us see if we can learn something from what we are shown*. We can tease out the meanings of dreams if we agree to be humble enough to sit with them and dwell for a while on our uncertainty.

113

Every day that I dream, I dream bigger.

Dreaming is like a channel between you and another world.[54] Each day that you can retrieve something from across that channel you have achieved a victory. Not all dreams will be eye-popping messages from the beyond, but keeping the line of communication open is an important achievement. Your attention to what comes through helps to reinforce the structure of the tunnel, as if you are securing the pathways to an underground mine. The more support structures and rail lines that we put in place, the more they help us to get the material out and, hopefully, the more stable the underground setting becomes. We do this by writing down our dreams, sharing them with others, reflecting on connections we can see between our dreams and our waking life, and valuing the dream as an important aspect of our decision making.

All these efforts allow us to dream bigger dreams. To get to the collective unconscious, we have to use that dream tunnel frequently. Much like you might practice a sport or lift weights for long-term benefits, dream recall practices allow you to remember more dreams, remember longer portions of dreams, and hence set you up to have the big dreams. Research suggests that in an eight-hour period of sleep, every person will have about four dream cycles. So, remembering only one dream a night is operating at a 25% retrieval rate. If you recall two or three dreams it is likely that at least one of those is going to be bigger than the other(s). Yet, we must also remember that dreams that might seem ordinary can have a big message. So set your intentions each night.

---

[54] Wolf, F.A. (1994). T*he dreaming universe: A mind-expanding journey into the realm where psyche and physics meet.* Simon & Schuster.

114

In a dream, no matter what other characters create or experience,
it all ends up being mine.

To dream is to observe new situations and reactions to unforeseen events. When bad things happen to other people in waking life, we do not benefit from their experience. We can take a sympathetic attitude toward what they experience such as *It sucks to be you*, or *You should have seen that coming.* If we are being told in a conversation about a third person, we also tend to be more judgmental: *She has been cruising for a bruising.* More rarely, we can adopt an empathetic attitude: *I can feel your pain.* However, this often occurs when we have gone through something already that is similar to what the person is experiencing. Typically, our Western world and its individualism feels little for our brothers and sisters. Even then, we get rewards for being "so kind."

Dreams differ because they automatically have an empathetic nature to them. In a dream, you are "in the action." It is all real to you, and you see that whoever is with you in your scenario seems to feel the exact same way: *We are in this together.* When you wake up from a dream and realize that none of this "really happened," then the question becomes *Why was it shown to me?* We cannot feel the same joy in personally escaping the trauma in the dream because it is only I who experienced anything (presumably, there are instances where two people shared the same dream). If we are all the characters, as Jung suggested, then we have a chance to practice feeling for our fellow brothers and sisters, known and unknown. Everything that happens is mine.

115

Dreams often transpose current psychological feelings from a particular
situation to a foreign situation, either historical or hypothetical.

Dreams are like a Rubik's cube of situations, scenarios, emotions, and actors. The dream scrambles them up and then sees how the action plays out. As a viewer of the dream, you are being put in the observer's role of a hypothetical situation. The waking value of a hypothetical situation is that the awake-me gets to try to reason out how one might act if they were in a similar situation later. The benefit of thinking about this is that we usually learn a bit about how our person thinks about the ambiguities that have been placed before them. A person's character is revealed by how they rationalize the actions that their dream-me performed compared to what their wake-me thinks it would do given the same situation.

The dream is a hypothetical situation for one. In a recent dream, I was casually betting five dollars on a swim team at a college swim meet. Some official overheard me and this violated the rules, causing the meet to be stopped to my great embarrassment. Any dream that elicits a strong emotion is likely to be a situation worth examining. What did you do right? What did you do wrong? How did you live up to your values (or not) and how are you stretched by the action of your dream-me? These are all questions for you to reflect on. Should something similar occur in waking life, you now have had a practice session. In my dream, I had to consider the fact that I had recently violated a somewhat serious unwritten rule because I had flippantly ignored it.

116

Dreams might show us what disembodied consciousness is like!
We can assume the "fly on the wall" perspective
or assume another person's identity.

Some reports of near-death experiences and astral projection suggest that consciousness can exist without the body. This is called disembodied consciousness. In these cases, consciousness is able to report details beyond what the body would be able to see. It can move to other locations and report details unavailable to the position of the body. In some dreams, we have similar experiences of consciousness. Instead of seeing the story of the dream through the dream-me's eyes (or point of view), we are given a bird's eye perspective, a selfless view of the actions. I refer to this as the third-person perspective, where we are witnessing our own body as an actor in the dream much like through a security camera.

The experience that consciousness is not always directly tied to the body might be a better depiction of how consciousness works. Many people experience the "hypnagogic hallucination" of falling through the mattress when they are about to "go under" during the falling-asleep period. This is a key component of "astral projection," where the body and consciousness are temporarily separated, and consciousness can travel to places without being embodied but also return to the body in a flash. I speculate that this is how dreams work as well since you always return to the same body no matter if you are in the POV or in the camera position.

117

I'm writing down this dream just to keep the rhythm.

Not every dream is going to be earthshaking. A dreamer might not think that there is much new information to be gleaned from the dream. I caution you not to judge a dream prior to writing it down. This is a mistake. First, even should it turn out that the dream yields nothing new, it is worth staying in the habit of writing down every dream that you can remember. In a sense, you are honoring the dream for arriving and strengthening your "reception" by letting all potential dreams know that you are ready to receive a communication and form of revelation if they are offering any. You are a humble recipient of their message and not someone who judges the message before you have transcribed it.

Second, I have found that "ordinary and unremarkable" dreams end up having a linguistically encoded message that is only uncovered when writing it down—the dream idiom. The way the dreamer describes the dream is more important than the plot. If the dreamer can compare their visual representation of the dream to common verbal idioms, then the message of the dream can yield that Ah-ha moment. The crux of dream work is writing down what you remember to keep the dreams coming.

It may help to think of yourself as a radio tower that receives incoming signals. The more time you put into talking to "those out there," the more that material will come to you because you are an open and receptive radio channel. You may have to listen to some of the same stories a few times for every great conversation, but those great conversations are worth the price.

118

Dreams cover the existential basics! They are intentional, relational, embodied, temporal, authentic (toward death), being there, and being there for others.

At least some dreams appear to be intentional, meaning they have a purpose, whether that is to instruct, warn, critic, or prepare the dreamer for something coming or something that recently occurred. Dreams are relational in that they use relationships that are familiar to us to reveal or focus us on some psychological experience. Dreams are embodied as dreams almost always contain us as human figures. Sometimes, of course, your consciousness is outside of your body, watching it from a distance, but you still know that is you. Dreams are temporal but time is fluid. You can appear as a child, teenager, college student, young adult, etc. It is rare for me to dream as an older person than I am.

Dreams are *authentic* in the sense that they can make us feel the uncanny (in Heidegger's sense[55]). Authentic means that we face our death frequently in dreams and then use it to contemplate our life. You will die many times in your dreams. Being there means to be actively engaged with presence in your life. Dreams certainly are action-based experiences; rarely do dreams focus exclusively on talking or inaction. One's dream-me is highly engaged in the action of the dream. Being there for others means that we are involved in helping or advancing the interests of other people. Certainly, we are often engaged in group activities where we play a part of a larger action and help or hinder the world of our and others' concern.

119

Dreams are wisdom opportunities because the dreamer has observational powers but not volitional powers.

Dreams can often provide example scenarios in which an approximate situation is presented that is similar to some current real-life event for the awake-me. The dream presents a "best available fit" example so that the unconscious is showing a simplified version of a more complex problem and providing guidance on how to act.

For example, a friend told me the following dream: he arrives at a specific place where there is supposed to be an open-gated parking lot. However, the gate is locked and posted outside are several "No Parking" signs. There are no other cars around. He senses he should not park there but overrules his feelings and does so anyway. When he returns, the parking lot is open, and it is completely full of cars. His car is

---

[55] Heidegger, M. (1962). *Being and time* (J. Macquarrie & E. Robinson, Trans). Harper Collins. (Original published 1926)

nowhere to be found. The parking attendant says that his car has been towed.

The dream here is not likely commenting on the parking behavior of this person. Most likely the dream is suggesting that the awake-me should pay attention to moments when there is a premonition to follow the rules. This hunch should not be overruled. In other words, the warning is that the person is going to encounter a situation when the details should be followed to the letter of the law. Otherwise, the results would be just as bad as having your car towed. It is the dreamer's responsibility to think about how this example is currently being lived out in waking life.

120

*We can dream together! When I dream of you,
do you ever dream of me?*

There have been several instances when two people dream of each other on the same night. This probably happens much more than we think, but we do not always reach out and tell that person our dream. Occasionally, two separate people will be speaking when they discover each had a dream that included the other. Even more rare, the first dreamer is surprised to find the second person recounts the same dream. This is definitely a synchronicity. This is sometimes called "mutual dreaming."[56] Not only does dreamer one dream of dreamer-two, but the scenario that occurs in the dream is eerily similar, if not identical.

Dreams can have a telepathic quality to them. Stanley Krippner showed in several experiments that dreams can be intentionally sent to people.[57] The experiment involved a person who was an experienced telepathic medium. The medium would be in a room several hundred miles away from the dreamer in a sleep laboratory. Once the dreamer entered REM sleep, the medium would be contacted and asked to open an envelope with a photograph. The medium was to send thoughts about the photograph telepathically to the dreamer, whose identity was not revealed. Before the dreamer completed their REM cycle, they

[56] Magallon, L.L. & Shor, B. (1990). Sharing dreams: Joining together in dream time. In S. Krippner (Ed.), *Dreamtime and dreamwork: Decoding the language of the night* (pp.252–260). Tarcher/Putnam.
[57] Davies, J.A., & Pitchforth, D. B. (2015). *Stanley Krippner: A life of dreams, myths and visions.* University Professors Press.

would be awakened and asked what their dream was about. A statistically significant number of dreamers gave reports of dreams that included major details from the photo sent telepathically by the medium.

121

I wonder if schizophrenia could be a sleep disorder
since a number of dream features, including the "suspension
of disbelief," seems to be present.

Some of the weird features of the dream world are that the extraordinary situations, the different rules of physics, and the incredible stretches in logic apply to this realm. No matter how strange the scenario is, the dream-me seems to go along with the parameters of the dream-maybe with the exception of death-it can take us to almost any unbelieve place, and we generally believe it.

Schizophrenia is a psychological disorder in which the person begins to have difficulty distinguishing the real from fantasy. People who experience this condition often see things that other people cannot see; they believe things that other people do not believe are happening. For example, someone might stare at the wall in horror. When asked what is happening, they claim the wall is bleeding, but you see none of that. They can claim to be people who they are not. Common examples include thinking they are Jesus or the Virgin Mary. No one agrees with their claims. Schizophrenia is considered a psychotic disorder—the most severe psychological illness we know.

I am struck by how similar the features of this disorder are to qualities of dreams. The ill person seems to have the same exact suspension of disbelief that the dreamer has. In a dream, the dream-me can be anyone, even Jesus, and they believe this totally. In dreams, unusual occurrences like bleeding walls happen all the time. Because of these commonalities, I have speculated that schizophrenia might be a "sleeping disorder."

122

Dreams can remind us that our life may still have another gear.

Dreams of a fantastic voyage or superpowers (e.g., ability to fly) can fill the dreamer with awe. These dreams may be speaking to untapped potential or "gifts" that one doesn't know one has. At some point in everyone's life, they need to be reminded about their own uniqueness. These dreams uplift the person emotionally in a way that an ordinary dream does not. Big dreams restore some faith that adventure is awaiting. Just as there are moments in life when we feel like the universe is working against us, these dreams can also remind us that sometimes the universe is working *with* us.

Another common way that dreams can tell us that we have further room to grow is through expanding the physical structures of some of our familiar homes. These dreams will often begin with having our dream-me in a very familiar room (e.g., own bedroom) in a childhood or current home. Then the dream-me will suddenly discover that there is a secret or hidden passage that the dreamer has never seen before. Upon opening this passage, the dream-me sees a larger room. For the most part, the room is almost completely empty.

I interpret this to mean that there is more space for you to grow. You may feel you have reached maturity and that you are complete and there is nothing left to accomplish. But this new room is there to fill up with your imagination. There is more to you than you thought, and now you can begin the "next chapter" in your life.

123

Dreams are spiritual because dreams displace the ego.

Maslow wrote about peak experiences in which one major aspect is that the ego is shrunk.[58]. This means that most of the time we see ourselves as the center of our world and everything that happens is either important or not involving our ego. When we climb to the top of a mountain or visit the vastness of the ocean at a beach, we subtly experience the vanishing of the importance of our ego. We see human activity as ant-like behavior compared to the vastness of the world. The world appears so much bigger than our daily concern.

The spiritual realm, as I think of it, is in a reciprocal relationship with the self. The more you are concerned with issues of the self, the less you can access the spiritual. To be truly present for spiritual moments, the self must be diminished. So graphically it might look like this: SELF ⇔ spiritual becomes SPIRITUAL ⇔ self. Spiritual moments

---

[58] Maslow, A.H. (1970). *Religions, values, and peak experiences.* Penguin Books Limited.

are individual because not everyone present at a mountaintop can let go of their ego.

Originally, the term "shrink" meant a psychologist who helped you see your concerns in a less egocentric fashion. By talking about one's problems, the client would discover they were not alone and that their problems were not the end of the world. I argue that dreams can also shrink our ego. Dreams take us out of familiar settings and challenge our sense of control. We can fly over and fall from mountains. We can travel to new lands and through time. These dreams seem to be a spiritual message encouraging us to see ourselves as a small, but significant, part of a greater whole.

124

My best prophetic dreams are only a year in the future.

Dreams can sometimes show you a future event. How far in the future you can be shown something and remember that you were shown it can be quite limited. My experience has been that most of the rare times that I recall having seen something in a dream that then came to pass was only a year prior to it happening. More recently, I had insights similar to dreams that revealed really interesting inventions. However, shortly after investigating the possible new invention, I discovered that someone else had already made and sold it. Again, it was less than a year between envisioning the object and the time of my discovery.

While I could be disappointed that I had such little lag time between insight and actuality, I do think it is good to know your dream timetable if you are serious about something that you have learned in a dream. Once you have observed the general time you have between dream and event, you now have an idea about how fast you have to move in order to get in front of the event happening. Most of my prophetic dreams have not been something that were big, significant occurrences. When the events did occur, the biggest shock was that they produced strong déjà vu feelings and chills. Probably 99% of my dreams have not come true, and that's a good thing. But if a dream seems prophetic or contains an invention, I now have a general idea about how fast I have to work on the intellectual property!

125

Dreams are the main way we learn to think about symbols.

Western school-age education has become more preoccupied by science, English, and math, leaving the arts behind and in almost all cases cutting arts programs whenever the first budget concerns arise. There is almost no help in learning about symbols and metaphors. It is as if the individual has to pick this up on their own through their native language, religion, or through the movies and reading. The West is very happy with a "what you see is what you get" mindset, where all we are interested in is just the facts.

The dream is one of the primary ways we are confronted by symbols.[59] A symbol usually appears as one thing but means something different. In dream talks, I describe a symbol as anything that does not fit with the times. So, using a sword in an era of guns is a symbol of something more. I have argued that animals are a common symbol used in dreams. We are familiar with animals, but we do not come in contact with most of them on a daily basis. A snake does not mean a real snake but more like symbolizes a person who is being deceitful. The dream contains these unusual elements, and we do not initially understand what they mean. In our confusion, we develop a deep desire to know what they are trying to tell us. Symbols allow us to step outside the literal bias of our culture and begin to search for different meanings beyond the sign. Dreams give us this nightly opportunity to practice symbolization.

126

The dream world is the parallel universe
that we keep believing might be out there.

Our galaxy has one inhabited planet with conscious beings on it. It is estimated that there are likely at least 100,000 possible inhabitable planets in our galaxy. Then there is something like two billion other galaxies. So, it seems possible that just like identical twins, two of the galaxies are close to being identical. Could it be that our awake-me experiences this real world, and our dream-me experiences the parallel, but not quite the same, world. Perhaps, we are connected like twins, who have a well-known "twin sense" about what is happening to the other. Or maybe we humans are more like the quark in quantum

---

[59] Fromm, E. (1951). *The forgotten language: An introduction to the language of dreams, fairy tales and myths.* (pp. 11-23). Grove Press.

mechanics that secretly seems to respond to the corresponding quark immediately, no matter the distance between them. In our dreams, we seem to experience this doubling effect.[60]

Our shadow appears to us as an inverse doppelgänger, typically exhibiting behavior that we find unbecoming. I have suggested that dreams contain double meanings and double entendres in which the linguistic description of the dream has two possible meanings: one a more literal definition and the other more metaphorical. Think of this as the connotation and denotation: a pig can literally mean a farm animal, but we also use that term to mean the police, an overindulging individual, and a male chauvinist. Generally, dreams are not literal.

127

In dreams, we experience the relationship between self, world, and others with great fluidity. Whereas in the waking world we try to objectify those relationships.

The waking world likes to objectify relationships. This means turning something into an object that is really a process. Mostly we objectify ourselves by stating that we are the type of person who will *always* do things the same way. We never are different but a thing or a machine that has been perfectly programmed. We objectify others, most famously in turning others into sexual objects. This means we do not see the person's character, only their body. We call other people schizophrenics and felons. The world, too, is often labeled as evil or corrupt or chaotic. All of these are simplifications that we like because they reduce the need to make complex decisions on a daily basis.

Dreams are more process oriented, meaning you have to look at the entire thing and not just one aspect. Hence, there is a greater fluidity and less objectifying. When our shadow appears in a dream, we say "Of course, I could never kill someone." But this, too, is an objectification of ourselves. The likelihood is that under the right conditions (e.g., defending our child), we are capable of such actions.[61] Dreams can put us in this position. Our relationships are challenged as many of our dreams include mother, father, and siblings in a whole array of different

---

[60] Wolf, F.A. (1994). *The dreaming universe: A mind-expanding journey into the realm where psyche and physics meet.* (pp. 256-263). Simon & Schuster.

[61] Underwood, J., & Bargdill, R. W. (2016). Consciousness. In R. Bargdill & R. Broome (Eds.), *Humanistic contributions to Psychology 101: Growth, choice and responsibility.* (pp. 43–62). University Professors Press.

interactions that show them in both sympathetic and unforgivable situations. Dreams about our world can show it as a hellscape or a utopia. The impossible is always possible in the dream, and we accept it there.

128

The more I study my dreams, the more I can live for a few moments in the "dream aether" on this side of consciousness.

Western civilization has spent almost 3,000 years trying to make everything known to the collective rational-mind network. Once something is known, it can be further studied and broken apart into pieces—much like our bodies, which are really one whole piece but segmented into hands and feet and organs and skin. Researchers become experts in these parts, and somehow the whole is largely forgotten. We no longer go to see a generalist but have to go see our dermatologist or eye doctor. Dreams seem to give us back this holistic view of life by presenting all things, everywhere, at once.

Sometimes we can be so caught up in a thought that we can be oblivious to outside circumstances (e.g., someone has to address us by name to get our attention). We have our head in the clouds and that means we are in the "aether," liminal, or numinous space where our sole focus is captivated by what we are dwelling on. Our dreams can pull us into a similar aether, where all logic and laws of the real world are broken. But this same aether occasionally is experienced as *flow* when we are fully engaged in a problem or activity. We can seemingly "lose time" and forget what we were moving through the world to do. Insight and dreaming share this sense of total engagement. The more we contemplate our dreams, the more we have the possibility of entering this liminal space while awake. This is the stream of consciousness or zone of instantaneous, creative magic!

Index

Note: Index based on Maxim Number, not on page number.

Index Based on Maxim Number.

About the Author

Richard Bargdill received his PhD in Clinical Psychology from the Existential Psychology program at Duquesne University in Pittsburgh, PA. He is currently an Associate Professor of Psychology at Virginia Commonwealth University. Dr. Bargdill is the author, co-editor and editor of four other books: *An Artist's Thought Book: Intriguing Thoughts about the Artistic Process*; *Humanistic Contributions to Psychology 101: Growth, Choice, and Responsibility*; *Living the Good Life: A Psychological History* (2nd Edition); and *Open a Window: An Artbook from Therapists*. His professional journal publications cover topics such as boredom, depression, meaning making, and the differences between fate and destiny. He has over two dozen published poems and his artwork dons the cover of five books including: *Silent Screams* and Andy Giorgi's *Reflections*. In addition to studying dreams, he is currently researching the assassination of environmentalists, aesthetic chills, and using the I Ching as a personal growth tool.

www.ingramcontent.com/pod-product-compliance
Lightning Source LLC
Chambersburg PA
CBHW050655270326
41927CB00012B/3042